ETHAN FROME

A Nightmare of Need

TWAYNE'S MASTERWORK STUDIES

Robert Lecker, General Editor

ETHAN FROME

A Nightmare of Need

Marlene Springer

TWAYNE PUBLISHERS • NEW YORK
Maxwell Macmillan Canada • Toronto
Maxwell Macmillan International • New York Oxford Singapore Sydney

Twayne's Masterwork Studies No. 121

Ethan Frome: A Nightmare of Need
Marlene Springer

Twayne Publishers   Maxwell Macmillan Canada, Inc.
Macmillan Publishing Company   1200 Eglinton Avenue East
866 Third Avenue   Suite 200
New York, New York 10022   Don Mills, Ontario M3C 3N1

Library of Congress Cataloging-in-Publication Data

Springer, Marlene.
    Ethan Frome : a nightmare of need / Marlene Springer.
        p.   cm.—(Twayne's masterwork studies; no. 121)
    Includes bibliographical references and index.
    ISBN 0–8057–9437–9—ISBN 0–8057–8586–8 (phk).
    1. Wharton, Edith, 1862–1937. Ethan Frome. I. Title. II. Series.
PS3545.H16E737   1993   92–42509
813'.52—dc20   CIP

10 9 8 7 6 5 4 3 2 1 (hc)
10 9 8 7 6 5 4 3 2 1 (pb)

Printed in the United States of America

For Ann and Rebecca

Contents

Illustrations

Note on the References
and Acknowledgments

References to *Ethan Frome* throughout this text are from the New American Library Signet Classic Edition, 1986. I am indebted to the Beinecke Library, Yale University, for permission to reproduce the photographs of Edith Wharton. Quotations from the play *Ethan Frome*, dramatized by Owen and Donald Davis, are reprinted by permission of the author and the Watkins/Loomis Agency.

I would like to thank Dr. Aimee Wiest and Dr. Erwin Hester for their careful reading of the text. Their insightful comments were extremely helpful. My gratitude too is extended to the members of my immediate staff at East Carolina University, whose patience, tactful protection of my calendar, and careful typing of the manuscript helped make this book possible. To my children, other family, and friends, whose support I shall always cherish, I give especial thanks, for they always help me through my own "granite outcroppings."

Edith Wharton, 1911

Yale Collection of American Literature, Beinecke Rare Book and Manuscript Library, Yale University

Chronology: Edith Wharton's Life and Works

1862	Edith Newbold Jones born 24 January in New York City, third child of George Frederick Jones and Lucretia Rhinelanders. Parents belong to wealthy, socially prominent New York families.
1866	Family moves to Europe for six years' stay in France, Germany, and Italy. During residence in Germany Edith suffers a severe attack of typhoid.
1872–1873	Family returns to United States and divides time between homes in New York City and Newport, Rhode Island, where Edith is active in the wealthy social scene.
1876–1877	Writes 30,000-word novella, "Fast and Loose."
1878–1879	Mother publishes Edith's *Verses,* a volume of 29 poems, and William Dean Howells publishes one of her poems in the *Atlantic Monthly.*
1880–1882	Busy with social seasons after debut in 1879. Is courted by a member of her social set, Henry Stevens. The engagement is announced in 1882, but broken off shortly thereafter. Father dies in 1882, leaving her a $20,000 trust fund.
1883	Spends summer in Maine. Begins a lifelong friendship with Walter Berry, a 24-year-old Harvard graduate who later becomes an international lawyer. In August Edith meets Edward (Teddy) Wharton, a 33-year-old Harvard graduate who lives on a $2,000 annuity from his family while he pursues his interests in camping, hunting, fishing, and polo.
1884	Hires Catherine Gross as her personal attendant. She will be Wharton's companion and housekeeper until her death 49 years later.

1885–1888   Marries Teddy Wharton on 29 April 1885 in New York City. Inherits $120,000 from a New York cousin, making her independently wealthy for life. In 1888 the Whartons spend their annual income on a three-month-long yacht cruise on the Aegean.

1889–1892   Whartons purchase a house in New York City. Four poems accepted by *Scribner's, Harper's Monthly,* and *Century Illustrated Monthly Magazine.* Short story, "Mrs. Manstey's View," published by *Scribner's* in 1891. Edith suffers intermittently from nausea and fatigue of undetermined origin. In 1892 she completes her novella "The Bunner Sisters."

1893–1898   Years of intermittent illness, including intense exhaustion, nausea, depression. Suffers a mental and physical breakdown in August of 1898 and is treated by S. Weir Mitchell, whose famous "rest cure" was popular among those who could afford it.

1899–1900   *The Greater Inclination* (short stories) published. *The Touchstone* published. Depression continues. Divides time between Europe, New York, Newport, and Lenox, Massachusetts.

1901   Whartons build The Mount, a hotel-sized mansion in Lenox, Massachusetts. *Crucial Instances* (short stories) published. Mother dies, leaving Edith a large trust fund.

1902   Edith's illness continues. *The Valley of Decision* and her translation of Sudermann's *Es Lebe das Leben* published. Meets Henry James and begins a long friendship and friendly rivalry with the noted author.

1903   *Sanctuary* published. Leisurely travels in Italy. Sells home in Newport. Teddy Wharton also suffers from mental breakdown.

1904   Purchases her first automobile. With Teddy driving, they take an extended tour of Europe and England. Hires Charles Cook, who will stay with Edith for the next 17 years, as a chauffeur. *The Descent of Man* (short stories) and *Italian Villas and Their Gardens* published. Returns to The Mount after travels and entertains a large array of houseguests.

1905   *Italian Backgrounds* and *House of Mirth* published, the latter receiving wide acclaim, with 140,000 copies in print by the end of the year. The Whartons dine at the White House.

1906–1907   *Madam de Treymes, The Greater Inclination,* and *The Fruit of the Tree* are published. Whartons move their winter home from New York to Paris. Edith writes the early sketch in French of *Ethan Frome*. Summers are spent at The Mount. Meets Morton Fullerton in Paris, and he in turn visits at The Mount.

1908   Teddy's mental health deteriorates. Edith visits Henry James in London. *The Hermit and the Wild Woman* and *A Motor Flight through France* published. Wharton begins affair with Fullerton.

1909–1910   Publishes *Artemis to Actaeon*. Moves to 53 Rue de Varenne in Paris and remains there for the next 11 years. Teddy is living in Boston. He later admits to embezzling $50,000 of Edith's money and using it to establish his mistress in Boston. Affair with Fullerton comes to painful end. Travels to England to see an ailing Henry James. Begins *Ethan Frome*. *Tales of Men and Ghosts* published. Teddy agrees to enter a Swiss hospital for treatment of depression.

1911   *Ethan Frome* serialized in *Scribner's* from August through October and published in book form in September. Well received both in America and Europe. Edith and Teddy formally separated. Edith gives Teddy power of attorney to sell The Mount.

1912–1913   *The Reef* and *The Custom of the Country* published. After much mental anguish, Edith divorces Teddy on 16 April 1913. Travels through Europe with Walter Berry, Bernard Berenson, and other friends.

1914   Continues travels in Europe and Africa with Percy Lubbock, Gaillard Lapsley, and Walter Berry and goes to England to see Henry James. Returns to Paris to organize war relief by establishing American Hostels for Refugees.

1915–1916   Publishes *Fighting France, The Book of the Homeless,* and *Xingu and Other Stories*. Henry James dies in 1916. Continues her war relief efforts. Made a Chevalier of the Legion of Honor, the highest award in France, for her work with refugees.

1917   *Summer,* the companion piece to *Ethan Frome,* published. Makes a month-long tour of Morocco with Walter Berry, where they visit a harem.

1918–1920   Buys Pavillon Colombe near Paris. Publishes *The Marne, French Ways and Their Meaning, The Age of Innocence,* and *In Morocco*. Under some financial pressure because of war relief efforts, her support of a financially troubled relative, and the

	effects of American income tax, but novels and stories continue to sell well.
1921	Awarded the Pulitzer Prize for *The Age of Innocence*.
1922–1923	*The Glimpses of the Moon* (screenplay by F. Scott Fitzgerald) published. Wharton awarded an honorary doctorate from Yale and returns to America for a short visit. *A Son at the Front* published.
1924–1926	*Old New York, The Mother's Recompense,* and *The Writing of Fiction* published. *Here and Beyond* (short stories) and *Twelve Poems* published.
1927	Walter Berry dies. She writes to a friend: "No words can tell of my desolation. He had been to me in turn all that one being can be to another, in love, in friendship, in understanding." *Twilight Sleep* published.
1928	Teddy Wharton dies. *The Children* published.
1929–1930	*Hudson River Bracketed* and *Certain People* (short stories) published. Wharton's health declines.
1931–1932	*The Gods Arrive* published. Begins autobiography, *A Backward Glance.*
1933–1934	*Human Nature* (short stories) and *A Backward Glance* published. In 1933 Catherine Gross, Wharton's companion of 49 years, dies. In 1934 Wharton tours England and Scotland.
1935–1936	*The World Over* (short stories) published. *Ethan Frome,* dramatized by Owen and Donald Davis, tours U.S. after successful run in New York.
1937	*Ghosts* (short stories) published. Wharton dies on 11 August 1937 after suffering a stroke. She is buried next to ashes of Walter Berry at Versailles. Her papers are left to Yale University Library, but closed to the public until 1969.

LITERARY AND HISTORICAL CONTEXT

The Mount

Yale Collection of American Literature, Beinecke Rare Book and Manuscript Library, Yale University

1

Historical Context

Unlike Edith Wharton's other major novels, the historical context of *Ethan Frome* is more deeply personal than decidedly public. Set in the stark hills of Massachusetts, the book's focus varies from Wharton's usual interest in wealthy turn-of-the-century Americans of her own social set who divided their time between New York, Newport, and the Continent.

Wharton was born in 1862 into a socially prominent New York family, which could, and often did, trace its lineage back to the early Dutch and English settlers of New York. Assured of a place in "Old New York" society by her parentage and her wealth, Edith was educated by governesses (she could speak three languages by age seven) and made her social debut at age 17—a year earlier than most girls, as befitting her precociousness. Neither her mother nor her father was inherently intellectual, but her father did own an expensive library (largely unused by him), and her mother, after first bruising Edith's young ego with a scathing review of her initial attempts at writing, later supported her apprenticeship by having a volume of her poems privately printed when she was only 16 years old.[1]

With the exception of her intense desire to write, Edith's early years were unexceptional for a girl of her class. As she either enjoyed or indulged the social season, she spent much of her time with her close circle of friends, ultimately marrying one of them, Teddy Wharton, in 1885 when she was 23 years old. At first the marriage was ostensibly a happy one, even if the polo-playing dilettante (his most visible talent was fly-fishing) and the intellectually curious writer had little in common. But deep within Edith's psyche this incompatibility was taking its toll. She suffered two nervous breakdowns, in 1894 and in 1898. During the latter she subjected herself to the popular cure prescribed by S. Weir Mitchell. The prescription of six weeks of total isolation, with complete bed rest, even to the exclusion of reading, had the same deleterious effects that it later had on Virginia Woolf, but fortunately with less serious results. Rather than committing suicide, Edith was able to relinquish her despair and turn even more seriously to her writing.

Edith had first attempted a novel at age 11 and published her first work, a short poem, at age 13. The first of what was to be 86 short stories, "Mrs. Manstey's View" was published in 1891, when she was 29. Her first masterpiece, *The House of Mirth*, appeared in 1905. In the course of her long career, spanning almost 60 years of writing with extraordinarily few fallow periods, Wharton would write 11 volumes of short stories, 17 novels, 7 novelettes, and numerous other books on interior design, the writing of fiction, and even a fascinating, if reticent, autobiography, *A Backward Glance*.

To write in such volume, Edith had to be as disciplined in her writing habits as she usually was in her life in general. She habitually worked each morning for three or four hours. She wrote in bed, in longhand, and gave the pages to Anna Bahlmann her secretary and friend to transcribe. Shortly after noon she would assume her role of formal host to what was a frequent array of guests and spend the afternoon and evenings in genial conversation over excellent cuisine—if she were not on one of her frequent trips.

In reading Wharton's biography one cannot help but be intrigued by what seems to be an endless succession of exciting journeys—to Morocco where she visited a harem, to Greece where she had to lower her car down a mountain with ropes, to the Aegean where she chartered a yacht for months of leisurely sailing, to Europe, to England—anywhere she had an urge to go—and always in the company of equally interesting friends: Henry James; Walter Berry, her friend of 44 years and a successful international attorney; Bernard Berenson, the editor and art connoisseur; Vernon Lee, the avant-garde author and critic; and many others. It was a life of delicate balance between industry and leisure, supported by inherited wealth and earnings from her writings and kept orderly by the dedication to duty and protection of taste that was so central to her culture and her fiction.

Such a well-mannered and measured world hardly seems conducive to the harshness of *Ethan Frome,* or even the inevitable tragedy that is so pervasive in her other work. But the imperious crispness of Wharton's outward appearance belied a passionate struggle within to maintain that order—a struggle that Wharton usually won, but, to her credit, occasionally lost. For, as Wharton's letters subtly reveal, she knew that a dedication to the preservation of culture and a sense of responsibility to a morality beyond self-interest, though noble goals, do not protect from the slings and arrows of outrageous fortune. And though the intellectual stimulation and emotional support of friends are necessities, they do not replace the need for an exclusive, compatible commitment between two people. Wharton was keenly aware that happiness, even when bolstered by material prosperity and friends, is an elusive luxury and that the human condition is often infused with circumstances that lead to loss, tragedy, and despair. It is from this deep understanding of human frustration and suffering that *Ethan Frome* was born.

Ethan Frome was written in 1910, the year she permanently settled in Paris and in many ways cut her ties with Americans forever. Personally, her life was in chaos. Her lifelong friendship with Berry was strained, later to be seamlessly repaired (she was buried next to him 27 years later). Teddy Wharton, increasingly subject to mental illness that made his behavior toward her both dramatic and demeaning, was a source of constant concern and frustration. They were to divorce in 1913 after a protracted struggle on Edith's part to gain her rights to her own income, then denied under United States marriage laws. The poverty of her own marriage was made even more evident to Edith when she fell passionately in love with someone else, Morton Fullerton. The affair with Fullerton, recorded by Edith both in letters and in erotic lyrics, lasted for three years, but because of her marriage and his demonstrated inability to make a lasting commitment to anyone, their relationship was a mixture of ecstasy and exasperation. Nonetheless, it opened Edith's eyes to both what could be and what could have been. And, as is so painfully evident in her stories of this time, when the affair ended in 1910, she learned firsthand the lessons of loss—the loss that infuses *Ethan Frome.*

After *Ethan,* Wharton went on to do some of her greatest work. *The Custom of the Country* was published in 1913 and *The Age of Innocence,* for which she won the Pulitzer Prize, appeared in 1920. World War I intervened, and Wharton organized a major refugee relief effort in Paris, for which she was awarded the Legion of Honor. The novels and short stories continued to come, as well as a critical piece, *The Writing of Fiction* (1925), and her autobiography, *A Backward Glance* (1933). When she died on 11 August 1937, she was working on an unfinished novel, *The Buccaneers.* Through this long career, Edith regularly drew on her memories of the Old New York of her youth or the immediate experiences of warring Europe. As time and distance increasingly separated her from both settings, she was occasionally accused of losing touch with the world of her fiction and of being insulated from the world around her. There is little doubt that Wharton's fictional and actual worlds are rarefied ones. She drew from the nonmoneyed world of Ethan only two other times, in "The Bunner Sisters" (1892) and *Summer* (1917), which she described in letters to Gaillard Lapsley as a "hot *Ethan.*" But Wharton did not pretend to be a newspaper reporter of her time, deliberately choosing instead to be retrospective and imaginatively introspective as the world changed around her.

Wharton was born at the end of one war and died on the eve of another. The United States was in the process of a total transformation. Her own New York grew from a city of 500,000 in 1850 to 3,500,000 by 1900. The robber barons irrevocably changed the course of American industry and New York society. In the 1870s, Boss Tweed took municipal corruption to new lows as he looted the New York City treasury. The labor movement, though not to get the right to strike until the 1930s, was fermenting in the dangerous factories and coal mines across the nation. The first continental railroad was completed in 1869, dramatically stimulating both industrial and agricultural productivity. America's participation in World War I made it a world power, if a reluctant one, and shifted American focus to an international setting, just as Wharton traveled from New York to Europe and other areas of the world. Women gained the right to vote in 1920, and by this time the automobile also became economically accessible, affording Americans a mobility previously unimagined. (Edith purchased her first car in 1904 and hired a permanent chauffeur.) Einstein challenged the limits of science, while Marx was doing the same for political and economic structures, and Freud for the human personality. By Wharton's death in 1937, the old order, however defined, had ended, and "the modern temper" was well ensconced.

Wharton, of course, observed and participated in all of these transitions, but they are relevant to *Ethan Frome* only in that the demands and pulls on the human heart that were motivated by them are pertinent to any age. Nonetheless, the writing of *Ethan,* and its subsequent history as both a novel and a play, are vital to Wharton's own journey as an artist. She acknowledges that *Ethan* was an important passage in her life: "It was not until I wrote 'Ethan Frome' that I suddenly felt the artisan's full control of his implements. . . . The book to the making of which I brought the greatest joy and the fullest ease was *Ethan Frome.*"[2] It is also the novel that clearly illustrates the eclecticism of Wharton's life and work: originally started in French as a lesson to polish and enlarge her vocabulary, it shows her bilingualism; set in Starkfield rather than Newport or Paris, it indicates her ability to imaginatively transcend her own life; a relentless tragedy, it captures the bleakness that infuses so much of her work; and, as a critically and financially successful play, it embodies both the drama of her work and the lasting appeal to audiences who were experiencing the rapid social changes taking place after 1911.

Teddy Wharton with his dogs, 1886

Yale Collection of American Literature, Beinecke Rare Book and Manuscript Library, Yale University

2

Importance of the Work

Ethan Frome is important to Wharton's canon because it represents her confident coming of age as an artist. *The House of Mirth*, published in 1905, could easily have convinced a less demanding writer of her worth, but it took this small novella, placed out of her usual milieu and using a personally atypical narrative technique, to assure Wharton that she could venture with success into areas beyond her immediate social strata and familiar settings. The success of *Ethan Frome* also showed Wharton that her strength as a stylist would support her in imaginative territory drawn from emotional empathy rather than familiar heritage. Consequently, the book is an excellent example of how a fine artist can creatively construct a believable story from vicarious observation and projection. Edith never had, nor ever would, live in a small, barren house bereft of heat and space, beauty and leisure, yet she had other deep connections to the loneliness that is Ethan's world.

Ethan Frome was conceived at a time when Wharton's own life was in chaos, and when the world around her was in such flux that neither personal nor public history offered much permanence. In such times, it is inviting to idealize stability and to romanticize the past. Wharton did neither. In her historically placed novels contemporary with *Ethan* she turns a sharp satiric eye on the Old New York of her heritage, exposing its opulence and its adoration of the status quo for the moral bankruptcy they represent. In *Ethan,* she once again refuses to accept setting at face value and exposes the poverty and harshness that the New England countryside could contain. Unlike other regionalists of her time (e.g., Sarah Orne Jewett), she rejected the accepted pretense that New England was entirely a country of pointed firs and neat cottages, preferring instead a realism in the mode of the bleak stories of Theodore Dreiser and Ellen Glasgow. And, in this novel too, Wharton depicts lives that offer order as the principal solace to searingly prove that predictability in itself is not necessarily a virtue. When readers first see Ethan, they are acutely aware that his life, as well as Mattie's and Zeena's, has plodded along with little variability for more than 20 years. Even if Ethan "lives to be the hundred" forecast for him, there will be little likelihood of change in the endless years ahead. Ethan has limped through his life; Mattie cannot move; and Zeena is chained to both. By drawing such people in such an existence, Wharton could write out her own fears of what her own emotional life, even if protected physically by money, could become if she did not risk change. The novel thus serves as a catharsis for her own anguish, as well as a test for her own skills as a stylist.

But what else does the story tell the reader, especially those of us not likely to be thrust into Ethan's poverty, to share his lack of education, or even to face the rigid social strictures that gave Edith Wharton her own sense of empathy with Ethan's lack of opportunity? In short, what basic questions about the human condition are raised by *Ethan Frome?*

First, *Ethan* offers us a stark realization of what life can be like if you accept circumstances with resignation—refusing, for whatever reason, to look at the variety of moral options to its dilemmas. Consequently, inherent in Wharton's story is the notion that an examined life will require risk and that though there is always a possibility of failure, to refuse to venture does not offer safety. Second, *Ethan Frome* disturbingly explores the possibility that life can offer equally strong conflicting choices: perceived duty versus genuine love; personal happiness for two versus righteous loneliness and penury for one;

the pressure of social structures versus the particularly American desire to "light out for the territory" as Huckleberry Finn and Ishmael did before Ethan. There is no decisive clarity of desire within Ethan, and he becomes frozen in his nightmare—a terrifying prospect for us all.

On a more positive level, *Ethan Frome* graphically illustrates that no matter how bleak our surroundings, no matter how grueling our labor, no matter how entwined we are with our environment, there exists in all of us a need for love, a desire to connect with another human being in a way that is self-sustaining and nurturing, that defines our own existence through intimate interaction with another person. Mattie becomes this person for Ethan, and he for her. His new joy in her presence, their mutual awareness that without each other they are not whole people, that life apart is not life at all, are strong testimony to the value of intimacy. That they would choose suicide over separation gives commitment its ultimate statement of worth.

But Mattie and Ethan are not allowed the luxury of death—and here perhaps is the most compelling aspect of *Ethan Frome*. For while Ethan and Mattie's initial love for each other tells us what we want to happen, their turn from love to bitterness tells us what can be. In the real world, the cowboy does not always get the girl; the ending is not happily ever after. The terror of *Ethan Frome* is that it could be truth; the truth of *Ethan* is that even if it is, one cannot live always fearing it will be. To live a life without a place for the heart, to live a life without beauty, without intellectual stimulation, is no life at all. For a variety of reasons—and therein lies the complexity of the story—Ethan, Mattie, and Zeena are left with such a life. By examining the emotional intricacies of how such a situation can evolve, the reader gains perspective on how to escape such a fate—to become, if at all possible, one of the "smart ones who gets away."

Ethan Frome has gained its place as a masterpiece of American literature for its style: it is brilliant in its economy, clarity, and structure. It is important for its place in Wharton's own development as an artist: she took a strange setting and a different voice and made them her own. It is crucial for Wharton's growth as a person: she artistically looked emotional and intellectual sterility in the eye and rejected both in favor of divorce. More universally, the novel is also extremely revealing for what it says about the entangled web the psyche can weave, imprisoning us in ways that sometimes neither love nor need can break. And it is compelling for what it says about power: the power to leave; the power to dominate other people through manipulation of their weakness; the power of money; the power of will. Finally, it is important for the questions it raises as readers gauge their reactions to Zeena's hate, Ethan's impotence, Mattie's lightness of being. Do readers sympathize, embrace, reject, pity, or run? For the moral issues it confronts, for the horror it explores, for the values it rejects and accepts, for the lives it reveals, and for the stylistic ease with which it accomplishes all of these things, *Ethan Frome* will continue to be read and respected.

3

Critical Reception

When Henry James read *Ethan Frome*, he assured Edith "it is going to be a triumph." In a letter to Morton Fullerton (22 September 1911) discussing James and quoting his remark, she says, "I think it's the first unqualified praise I've ever had from him, and it does me good."[1] The story first appeared in three installments in *Scribner's Magazine* (August, September, and October 1911) and then in book form on September 30, selling for one dollar. The reviews were good, though the reviewers were often puzzled and consistently pained. The reviewer in the *Bookman* says, "It is hard to forgive Mrs. Wharton for the bitter remorselessness of her latest volume, *Ethan Frome*, for nowhere has she done anything more hopelessly endlessly grey with blank despair."[2] The *Nation*, however, records, "The wonder is that the spectacle of so much pain can be made to yield so much beauty. And here the full range of Mrs. Wharton's imagination becomes apparent."[3] The *New York Times Book Review* is not so laudatory, arguing that Wharton chooses to present life in its tragic aspects but without the deep sympathy and tolerance of the great novelists. This is, says the reviewer, a cruel, haunting story, "but it is a story which a bald telling, without the art which has thrown the crude material of the plot into due dramatic perspective and given its poetic atmosphere, could easily make absurd, or even revolting."[4] With perhaps more prescience than he knew, the reviewer concludes that Wharton is a dramatist who passes as a novelist. And the review in the *Outlook* somewhat snobbishly proclaims, "As a piece of artistic workmanship it would be hard to overstate the quality of this story; it is conceived and executed with a unity of insight, structural skill, and feeling for style which lies only within the reach of an artist who, like Guy de Maupassant, knows every resource of the art. It is to be hoped that when Mrs. Wharton writes again she will bring her great talent to bear on normal people and situations."[5] The reviewer does not define *normal*.

Edith was pleased with the book's reception but disappointed in the sales. In a letter to Charles Scribner of 27 November 1911, she expresses her concerns and accuses her publisher of 23 years of poor advertising. Scribner responded with a detailed account of the book's sales, but in May of that year she announced that she had given her next novel, *The Reef*, to D. Appleton & Company. Charles Scribner was disappointed but responded with gentlemanly decorum: "Nothing is more difficult to meet than the statement of an author's friends who report that a book is selling tremendously or cannot be had at the best bookstores. Retail clerks are very apt to say whatever they think a customer wishes to hear" (*Letters*, 263–64).

The subsequent critical reception of *Ethan Frome* has been a varied one, though recognition of its intrinsic worth has been sustained. There is little question that *Ethan Frome* has been continually recognized as one of Wharton's most important works. In his obituary article for the *Saturday Review,* Henry Seidel Canby notes, " 'The House of Mirth,' 'The Age of Innocence,' 'Ethan Frome,' and especially the two latter, justify all the honors which she was fortunate enough to receive in her lifetime. And they constitute an argument, if not a claim, for the future."[6] Percy Lubbock in "The Novels of Edith Wharton" argues, "Mrs. Wharton, in the few and simple pages of 'Ethan Frome,' has shown more conclusively that she possesses this power [to identify with her characters and thus channel their emotions] than in anything else she has written, for she has written nothing in which she has so rigorously denied herself all other help."[7] There were, certainly, dissenting critics. An influential one, William Lyon Phelps, in his book

The Advance of the English Novel, devotes three and one-half pages to Wharton, saying, "Mrs. Wharton is a good hater; if her sense of humor and her power of human sympathy were developed in like measures with her capacity for hate, disgust, and irony, what a novelist she would be."[8] He accuses her of lacking "heavenly powers." Phelps's lack of critical acumen is further illustrated by his view that "of all American authors who have made their debut in the twentieth century, I regard Mr. Henry Sydnor Harrison as the most promising" (Phelps, 285). (Harrison was a minor turn-of-the-century Southern writer whose six novels enjoyed momentary success; Phelps was later to relent somewhat and admit to the strength of *The Age of Innocence*.)

Agreeing with the more favorable critics, Edith admitted that *Ethan* was one of her favorites, and it is her only work to receive a personal introduction written for the Modern Student's Library edition of the novel in 1922. In this short essay she outlines two objectives: to give the reader "a statement as to why [she] decided to attempt the work in question, and why [she] selected one form rather than another for its embodiment."[9] As for why she attempted the work, Wharton argues that previous New England fiction bore scant resemblance to the harsh realities of the New England countryside and the harshness of people's lives there. Later, in *A Backward Glance,* she talks of the "rose-coloured spectacles of my predecessors, Mary Wilkins and Sarah Orne Jewett" (*BG,* 1002); she wanted to give a more realistic picture.

In addressing the question of form, Wharton knew her story presented problems of both dramatic tension and language: "how to deal with a subject of which the dramatic climax, or rather the anti-climax, occurs a generation later than the first act of tragedy," and how to fully outline the psychological depth of a situation when the characters themselves have a deep-rooted cultural reticence and inarticulateness. Wharton's answer to both problems was the narrator—a man who is more knowledgeable and sophisticated than the people around him and who shares and stimulates the reader's curiosity to know more about those he meets.

In this introduction, Wharton inadvertently raises two issues that would become important areas of controversy among critics of the work: setting and form. In defending her choice of setting, Wharton says in *A Backward Glance,* " 'Ethan Frome' was written after I had spent two years in the hill-region where the scene is laid, during which years I had come to know well the aspect, dialect, and mental and moral attitude of the hill people" (*BG,* 1004). She, too, however, was not oblivious to the irony of her circumstances. She wrote of the novel to Bernard Berenson (4 January 1911): "The scene is laid at Starkfield, Massachusetts, and the nearest cosmopolis is called Shadd's Falls. It amuses me to do that decor in the Rue de Varenne" (*Letters,* 232). Critics have been less amused, noting that Wharton's real vantage point for the New England she wrote about was The Mount, her mansion near Lenox, Massachusetts, an elegant house, surrounded by elaborate gardens and lawns and staffed by numerous competent servants. Abigail Ann Hamblen sums up her sense of Edith's choice with "Edith Wharton's approach to the Massachusetts 'hill country' savors decidedly of the air of an aristocrat going slumming among the lower orders."[10] There is little question that the setting is an unusual one for Wharton, yet one that she was drawn to perhaps by her sense of personal frustration with her life, regardless of its opulence, and because of a desire to strip the human personality to its barest external essentials and turn to the drama within the human mind.

By putting her setting in bas-relief, Wharton freed herself of her usual practice of dwelling on the furnishings of life and wrote of people moving in the negatives of life's snapshots rather than in the color of the photograph itself. In her Modern Library introduction, Wharton acknowledged her choice:

> The theme of my tale was not one on which many variations could be played. It must be treated as starkly and summarily as life had always presented itself to my protagonists; any attempt to elaborate and complicate their sentiments would necessarily have falsified the whole. They were, in truth, these figures, my *granite outcroppings;* but half-emerged from the soil, and scarcely more articulate. . . . [Ethan Frome] was the first subject I had ever approached with full confidence in its value, for my own purpose, and a relative faith in my power to render at least a part of what I saw in it. ("Intro.," 124)

Yet it is precisely Wharton's themes in the novel, and her decision to develop her characters sparsely, that have most perplexed her critics. The debate swirls around both theme and characterization. A year after Wharton's death, Bernard De Voto in his 1938 introduction to *Ethan Frome* says the novel is "not a transcript of human experience. . . . It is a well-made novel done with exact calculation and superb skill, but it is not an exploration of or comment on genuine emotion." For De Voto, however, craftsmanship compensates for theme, and he posits that Wharton was deliberately practicing detachment: "By flawless workmanship alone a professional writer has persuaded you to accept an essentially construed story."[11]

It was Lionel Trilling, however, who fired one of the most influential negative salvos and started a major critical debate when he declared in his excellent essay "The Morality of Inertia" that *Ethan Frome* "was a dead book, the product of mere will. What is more, it seemed to me quite unavailable to any moral discourse. In the concept of morality, there is nothing to say about *Ethan Frome.* It presents no moral issue at all." Trilling does argue, however, that the story contains an important idea: "That moral inertia, the *not* making of moral decisions, constitutes a very large part of the moral life of humanity." Ethan, thus, does not make choices; he merely responds to the dull unthinking round of daily duties. Nor can we see morality in Ethan and Mattie's fate: "Between the moral life of Ethan and Mattie and their terrible fate we cannot make any reasonable connection. Only a moral judgement cruel to the part of insanity could speak of it as anything but accidental." Wharton's novel, says Trilling, is not to be praised but should at least be recognized for bringing to our attention what we so often forget: "the morality of inertia often becomes the immorality of inertia."[12]

Irving Howe and E. K. Brown also agree with Trilling that it has little moral value and with De Voto that technique is the novel's primary strength. Howe calls the novel "a severe depiction of gratuitous human suffering . . . a work meant to shock and depress."[13] Brown maintains, however, that of all Wharton's works this one is the most certain to endure and calls it a "great technical experiment."[14]

Other critics, however, contend more persuasively that the novel does have a definite moral tone and that both characterization and plot are authentic. Blake Nevius sees Ethan's tragedy resulting from the "wasteful submission of a superior nature to an inferior one." The lingering taste of the story is the "despair arising from the contemplation of spiritual waste." Ethan is trapped into his death in life by his sentimental feeling of loyalty to Zeena for her devoted nursing of his mother. Through this scenario Wharton explores a central theme of her fiction: "What is the extent of one's moral obligation to those individuals who, legally or within the framework of manners, conventions, taboos, apparently have the strictest claim on one's loyalty?"[15]

Nevius also defends Wharton's choice of point of view and her disciplined style, attributing the latter to her friend Walter Berry's influence. In his support of Wharton's decision to use an outside narrator, Nevius disagrees with John Crowe Ransom who sees the narrator as intrusive and as evidence of Wharton's discomfort with both subject matter and setting: "Why a special reporter at all? And why such a peculiar chronological method? These are features which picture to me . . . the perturbation of an author wrestling with an unaccustomed undertaking, uneasy of conscience, and resorting to measures.[16] Like Nevius, Alfred Kazin is also troubled by the structure of the novel—"there is something mechanical and too obvious about the device framing the story"—but contends that we "easily overlook this under the spell of genuine human tragedy. . . . No reader can escape the emotional force of *Ethan Frome*." Kazin's praise of the novel, written in 1987, is a softening of his earlier position. In *On Native Grounds* (1942) he attacks Wharton for her condescension, saying, "she could conceive of no society but her own, she could not live with what she had . . . she knew little of the New England common world, and perhaps cared even less."[17]

With the publication of R. W. B. Lewis's definitive biography in 1975, interest in Wharton's work was revitalized. Lewis acknowledges his debt to Percy Lubbock's 1947 biography but quickly realized that Lubbock's picture of Wharton as an aloof stuffy grande dame was not accurate. Drawing on her letters, diaries, and previously undiscovered erotic poetry, Lewis reveals a woman who was naturally generous, spiritually kind, full of both passion and laughter, and had a "lifelong capacity . . . for deep and abiding friendship." Lewis also notes, perhaps with a touch of exaggeration, that *Ethan Frome* "is one of the most autobiographical stories ever written" (Lewis, xii, xiv). He has high praise for the novel, calling it a classic of realism and labeling it Wharton's most effectively American work. It is autobiographical, says Lewis, in that Ethan's final tragic situation, living out his life as a wreck of a man surrounded by whining people, is Wharton's appalling vision of what her life could ultimately become if she continued to stay with Teddy—a vision put into even starker relief by the happiness she was then enjoying with Morton Fullerton (Lewis, 310).

In the years following Lewis's biography, critical interest in Wharton grew. In the next decade, at least 18 doctoral dissertations focused on her work and at least six book-length studies appeared, all taking an innovative approach to her work. For example, Gary Lindberg, in *Edith Wharton and the Novel of Manners* (1975), analyzes *The Custom of the Country, Ethan Frome, The House of Mirth,* and *The Valley of Decision,* maintaining that her novels are accounts of characters operating within an unexpectedly troubling network of habits and patterns of behaviors that constitute a defined culture. Lindberg argues that Wharton constructs her plots "so as to undermine the protagonists' moments of expansive meditation by developing early the very forces that will frustrate their expectations. . . . Ethan's hopes are doomed before they are recognized, and this is one reason the novel seems harshly fatalistic." Margaret McDowell's *Edith Wharton* (1976) is a helpful introductory survey of the major novels but concentrates on those written after 1920. Richard Lawson's *Edith Wharton* (1977), also an introductory study, concludes that Wharton's special gifts are in setting and style and draws convincing parallels between Wharton's life and Ethan's.[18]

The two most important studies to appear after Lewis' seminal work, however, are Cynthia Griffin Wolff's *A Feast of Words: The Triumph of Edith Wharton* (1977), a critical biography that builds on Lewis and takes a psychoanalytic look at Wharton's life and canon, and Elizabeth Ammons's *Edith Wharton's Argument with America.*[19] In her complex work, Wolff explores the ramifications of Wharton's early rejection of her mother, which resulted both in a "failure of trust, a voracious need for human comfort that carried with it a cosmic conviction of inevitable disappointment," and in a need to communicate those feelings of distrust and disappointment to the world at large (Wolff 1977, 14). In her excellent section on *Ethan Frome,* Wolff argues that the structure of the novel is the true subject of the tale and that Wharton uses the narrator to explore her own fears of repressing all feeling in favor of a peaceful, stultified existence. Repression is seen as an existential necessity for life. While Wharton was writing from this place within herself, her fictions are worlds of unrelieved desolation. With the writing of *Ethan Frome,* Wharton was able to recognize the horror for what it was and to reject it.

Ammon's book continues in the psychoanalytic vein but sees *Ethan Frome* as a fairy tale, drawing on the archetypes of the genre: the witch, the silvery maiden, the honest woodcutter. The tale is terrifying because here the witch wins. Moreover, the narrator exposes the deepest psychosexual level of *Ethan Frome* by identifying with Ethan in realizing a deep male fear: that woman will turn into witch, that "mother will turn into witch, love into hate, day into night, life into death." Like Wolff, Ammons extends her analysis to illustrate how Wharton writes about her own fears of maternal rejection, which lead to fear of female betrayal in general. First Ethan's mother abandons her caretaking of him, then Zeena does the same. Mattie is not a maternal figure, and she—horribly—turns into Zeena. "The tale looks at man's romantic dream of feminine solace and transport and, with a hideous twist, allows Ethan's fantasy to materialize. . . . The two witchlike women hold him prisoner for life in the severely limited economy and social landscape that traps all three of them" (Ammons, 74–75).

Carol Wershoven's *The Female Intruder in the Novels of Edith Wharton* (1982) is exemplary of the careful attention feminist scholars, building on the work of Wolff and Ammons, have continued to give to Wharton's work. Wershoven notes that many of Wharton's novels, including *Ethan Frome,* contain a female intruder, a character who stands outside her society and functions by forcing other characters to reexamine their world. This female intruder points out to other female characters how trapped they are, teaches protagonists alternative ways to live, reproaches false social values, forces readers to judge society in her terms, and exemplifies Wharton's own values.[20]

The modern study of Wharton's psychoanalytic history initiated by Lewis's biography and so brilliantly supplemented by Wolff and Ammons has also continued, with one of the most recent full-length studies focusing not on Wharton's mother, as did Wolff's, but on her father. David Holbrook, in *Edith Wharton and the Unsatisfactory Man*, pushes the therapist's approach to its critical limits as he takes a distinctively Freudian approach to Wharton's childhood and to her development as an artist. Drawing heavily on Wharton's extant pornographic fragment, "Beatrice Palmato," Holbrook speculates that Wharton was abused by her father as a child and that the experience twisted her view of sexuality and became "a mainspring of her art." In Wharton's novels, her characters are in pursuit of a relationship through which they can define their own uniqueness. The quest is doomed to fail, for all the men in Wharton's heroines' lives fail their women, unless they are father figures. In the story of Ethan, the sleigh ride is a symbolic sexual act that "brings catastrophe and leads to perpetual misery."[21]

The most recent major contribution to Wharton biographic scholarship is the publication of R. W. B. and Nancy Lewis's edition of the letters. Much of Wharton's correspondence was destroyed. Her letters exchanged with Percy Lubbock and Geoffrey Scott are gone, Henry James burned almost all he received between 1902 and 1915, and she went to Walter Berry's apartment after his death in 1927 and burned the letters she found there. The letters to Morton Fullerton were also presumed lost until 300 of them were found in 1980. Nonetheless, more than 4,000 letters have survived. Scarcely a day passed, Lewis tells us, when she was in good health, that she did not write at least half a dozen letters; once she returned from a three-day trip to find 65 letters waiting for her. The largest surviving correspondences are with several editors at Scribner's and with Bernard Berenson, the historian and art connoisseur, and his wife Mary. The Lewises have done a remarkable job of cutting the 4,000 to 400 and presenting a coherent narrative, including concise biographical essays and assiduous annotations to weld the story. Here we see Wharton's own account of what Lewis had previously recorded in his biography: a woman who apparently suffered a nervous breakdown in 1894 at the age of 32 (there are no letters for 16 months), who recovered to become a prolific novelist. Her gratuitous reliance on extreme wealth is persuasively evident by the nonchalance in which she accepts being constantly cared for, acquiesced to, and having the luxury of infinite variety and choice in her life. Her frenetic traveling, her intense patriotism, her capacity for deep friendship, her passionate love for Fullerton are all here—as are examples of her business acumen, as she negotiates better and better contracts, and her vulnerability to critics. Wharton was a voluminous and skilled correspondent; the Lewises' collection does justice to her talent.

In addition to the full-length texts devoted to her work, Wharton's fiction has also received extensive critical attention in articles and reviews. They are too numerous to be detailed here but are readily available in libraries and are listed in several bibliographies of her work.

Early studies of Wharton's work focused on her style and, secondarily, on her content. Gradually, the focus has shifted—first to a clearer appreciation of Wharton as a writer who had a distinctive approach to one segment of the American character and then to a more accurate picture of Wharton as a person. With the opening of her papers at Yale, R. W. B. Lewis was able to correct the distorted view of Wharton as an arrogant, snobbish prude perpetrated by Percy Lubbock's biography. Because of Lewis's careful and caring work, we now have a portrait of the artist as a sensitive, shy, generous, and extremely complex woman. Other critics have followed Lewis's lead into Wharton's mind and work, tracing her creative history back through her mother, her father, her friends, and her lovers. Stimulated by the interest in women's literature and women's studies in general, feminist scholars have continued to find new insights in her eclectic canon. The Edith Wharton Society is also a significant force in nursing critical interest in Wharton's work. This study is clearly indebted to the work of all of these scholars, but finds its own truth somewhere between an appreciation of *Ethan Frome* purely for its technical virtuosity and the opposite critical attempts to categorize all of Wharton's work through her biography. It explores the importance of *Ethan Frome* to Edith Wharton but approaches each of her characters as separate people sitting at the same sparse table, acting out their dance of anger, love, frustration, and need. Ultimately, this study hopes to show why *Ethan Frome* is indeed a "feast of words."

4

Style

Above all else, Wharton's reputation as a master stylist, as a writer who devoted extraordinary care to technique, has remained sound. No novel presented her with more of a stylistic challenge than *Ethan Frome,* for not only was she writing out of her social and geographical milieu, but, as she says in her preface to the novel, she also had to depict characters noted for their "deep-rooted reticence and inarticulateness." Wharton realized her challenge but indicated that, by choosing to use a narrator, she not only overcame the limitations of the region's culture and her own familiarity with it, but also added new dimensions to the story.

Wharton agreed with Henry James that the location of point of view is the central difficulty of the novelist. She also shared James's preference for a reflecting consciousness, capable of comprehending the significance of the events witnessed. Ironically, James was not pleased with this anonymous narrator and gently chided Edith for her choice, noting that he had little resemblance to the author and had an inadequate connection to the story. In fact, James actually snickered at the narrator's statement that he "was sent by my employers," noting that the imperious Edith would scarcely be sent anywhere.[1] Fortunately, the novel was already in print, and well received, prior to James's comments. They affected Wharton more as a friend than as a writer.

In her preface to the novel, Wharton defends her choice of form: "Each of my chroniclers contributes to the narrative *just so much as he or she is capable of understanding* of what, to them, is a complicated and mysterious case; and only the narrator of the tale has scope enough to see it all, to resolve it back into simplicity, and to put it into its rightful place among his larger categories" ("Intro.," 1125).

Since some critics did chide her for her choice of structure, she countered in *A Backward Glance:* "I have pondered long on this structure, had felt its peculiar difficulties, and possible awkwardness, and could think of no alternative which would serve as well in the given case; and though I am far from thinking "Ethan Frome" my best novel, and am bored and even exasperated when I am told that it is, I am still sure that its structure is not its weak point" (*BG*, 941).

Wharton's defensiveness about *Ethan,* and her deprecating its importance to her, is slightly disingenuous here given her comment that in writing *Ethan* she had at last felt the artist's full control. Moreover, Wharton's own favorites have not had historical support. She considered her best to be *The Valley of Decision, The Gods Arrive, The Custom of the Country, Summer,* and *The Children* (Lewis, 490).

Wharton's choice of a filtering conscience was a determined one, done after an earlier attempt at direct narration; in her first version of the story there is no such character. As mentioned earlier *Ethan Frome* originated as an exercise to learn French. Wharton tells us in a brief article in *The Colophon:*

> The conditions in which *Ethan Frome* originated have remained much more clearly fixed in my memory than those connected with any of my other stories, owing to the odd accident in the tale's having been begun in French. Early in the nineteen hundreds I happened to be spending a whole winter in Paris, and it occurred to me to make use of the opportunity to polish and extend my conversational French; for though I had spoken the language since the age of four I had never had occasion to practice it for any length of time, at least with cultivated people, having frequently wandered through France as a tourist, but never

lived there for more than a few weeks consecutively. Accordingly, it was arranged that I should read and talk for so many hours a week with a young French professor; and soon after our studies began he suggested that before each of his visits I should prepare an "exercise" for him. I have never been able, without much mental anguish, to write anything but a letter or a story, and as stories come to me much more easily than letters, I timidly asked him if a story would "do," and, though obviously somewhat surprised at the unexpected suggestion, he acquiesced with equal timidity. Thus the French version of *Ethan Frome* began, and ploughed its heavy course through a copy-book or two; then the lessons were interrupted and the Gallic "Ethan" abandoned, I forget at what point in his career.[2]

The French copybook has survived, but the tale that it tells is very brief. In it there is a New England farmer named Hart, married to a sickly wife, Anna, and in love with his wife's niece, Mattie. Anna suddenly says that Mattie must leave. Hart offers to go with her, but Mattie, claiming that Anna has been kind to her, refuses his offer. Though the brief tale does contain the germ of the story as we now know it, and there are a few parallel descriptive passages, missing are two essential ingredients of the familiar story—the tragic accident or attempted suicide, and the narrator. Generally, the style in the French version is bad, the characters lack definition, and the ending is weak.[3]

In deciding to use a narrator, Edith tells us that she makes no claim for originality, that Browning's *"The Ring and the Book"* and Balzac's "La Grande Breteche" had set magnificent examples and that the chief merit here was to recognize the structural applicability. Balzac does indeed use the same device, with some difference. In Balzac's story, the narrator is distantly objective and does not elaborate on the tale. A notary, a landlady, and a maid all tell him parts of a story set in an old brown house on the banks of the Loire. It is a story of marital infidelity and murder, where the deranged and cuckolded husband has the lover of his wife walled up in a closet in her bedroom. The lover is left to starve to death while the bereaved wife is forced to sit helplessly beside her husband and listen to the lover die. Like *Ethan*, the setting for the story is grim, and each is a story of frustrated love. In Balzac, however, the degenerate husband, who suffers a miserable death from excesses of all kinds, garners the revenge. His wife dies, deranged, eaten by mortal disease until "she was nothing more than a phantom."⁴ *Ethan* and "La Grande Breteche" share narrative form, grimness of tone, and the theme of frustrated love, but little else. Balzac's tale is a horror story of the type made so familiar by Poe; Wharton's tale carries us much further into the human soul and the human dilemma.

The person Wharton chooses for her narrator is a man relatively unfamiliar with the region. He is urbane, intellectual, empathetic, and well educated. He has been sent by his employers to do an emergency job on a power house near Starkfield and is forced to remain longer than he anticipated because of a labor strike. Naturally curious, he is drawn into Ethan's story first when he sees Ethan at the post office and recognizes that he is "but the ruin of a man," yet has a "careless powerful look," with "something black and unapproachable in his face."⁵

Being almost hypnotically attracted to Ethan, the narrator leads us into Ethan's life. He tells us that he gets the story "bit by bit, from various people," and that "each time it is a different story" (*EF*, 3). From the opening line Wharton sets us up for an unusual telling. In the second paragraph a direct address to the reader ("If you know Starkfield, Massachusetts, you know the post office") establishes the conversational tone of the first person narrator, but we soon realize that the facts of the story will be hard in coming, for not only are the townspeople reticent to talk, but the narrative framework is deliberately obscure.

If one reads Wharton's story in two parts, first reading the two frame chapters, the first and last, one realizes how little is actually known about Ethan. The narrator tells us the story several years after he has learned it, and he hears of it 24 years after it has happened. This mixture of the general and specific gives an aura of veracity to the narrator's story, while still allowing the truth "the ragged edges" that Herman Melville notes as integral to complexity. The narrator gets the basics of his story from Harmon Gow, the stage driver. He learns that Ethan had a terrible accident 24 years ago come February and that Ethan had spent his youth caring for people: "Fust his father—then his mother—then his wife" (*EF*, 5). The narrator then tells us that Gow has taken the tale as far as his "mental and moral reach permitted" (*EF*, 6) but that the deeper meaning of the story was in the untold gaps.

In trying to fill the gaps, the narrator next queries his landlady, Mrs. Hale, the former Ruth Varnum. Usually a gregarious woman with a wealth of local lore, Mrs. Hale is "unexpectedly reticent" (*EF*, 8) on this topic, implying that the subject is too painful to discuss. The narrator returns to Harmon, learns a bit more in that Harmon tells him that Ruth was the first to see Ethan after the accident, and that Ethan is now in need of money and would welcome the chance to take the engineer to the station. Harmon apparently arranges the deal, for Ethan appears at the engineer's door the following morning, and the engineer's relationship with Ethan begins.

The trip to and from the station with Ethan merely whets the engineer's curiosity and adds little factual knowledge. We learn that Ethan has once been to Florida (like the engineer) and that he once had an interest in science, again like the engineer. After the engineer is invited into Ethan's house because of a snowstorm, we know that he lives with two women, his wife Zeena and Miss Mattie Silver. The narrator also learns that the L of the house, the physical connection between the house and barn, the symbolic link with work and nourishment, has been torn from Ethan's house and that the farm has deteriorated from his father's day. Everything in Ethan's life is moving despairingly backward.

The narrator enters Ethan's house, first into the hall, then into the kitchen. He then tells us he has a "vision" of his story, and an ellipsis follows; the story of Ethan's past begins. When the ellipsis ends, we are back at the beginning, entering the kitchen. Mattie and Zeena are old before their time, like Ethan. We learn that Mattie is soured, her face bloodless and shriveled. Zeena's pale opaque eyes reveal nothing and reflect nothing. The house is the Ancient Mariner's "death-in-life." Like the Mariner, the narrator recoils in horror, fleeing to the warmth of Mrs. Hale. Once again, however, Mrs. Hale gives little to substantiate the story we have just read. She is surprised that the engineer has been invited in and now reveals that she occasionally visits the Frome house—usually twice a year—to mark the new year and once in the summer. But she says Ethan's tragic face makes more frequent visits intolerable. Immediate time passes—we do not know how much, except that the engineer had returned in the morning and it is now night, with old Mr. Hale in bed, and the two are sitting alone. The narrator tells us: "Mrs. Hale glanced at me tentatively, as though trying to see how much footing my conjectures gave her; and I guessed that if she had kept silence till now it was because she had been waiting, through all the years, for some one who should see what she alone has seen" (*EF,* 130).

What these conjectures are, we never really learn. There is, however, some unspoken understanding between the two, for Mrs. Hale does lapse into a recollection of the tragic day, saying that she was with Mattie when she regained consciousness and that Mattie had looked at her to say something that the reader never learns, just as Mrs. Hale never knows what Zeena thought or why she took Mattie back to the farm. We are never to know for sure, but having read the narrator's version of the "gaps," we are convinced that Mrs. Hale is right when she says there is little difference between the Fromes who are alive and those who are dead.

What, then, are we to surmise about the narrative frame? We are told directly only the barest of details. The narrator assures us he has been told the story by several people, but unlike Balzac's narrator, we are never told how much he learns from whom. Mrs. Hale must have heard enough of the narrator's story to substantiate his "subsequent inferences" of the initial chapters and his "conjectures" of the concluding frame, for she trusts him with her judgment. Nonetheless, time, details, sources for the story, the usual stuff of narrators, are all deliberately blurred here; the reticence so integral to the culture is a metaphor for the technique also.

Recognizing that Wharton intentionally manipulates the vagueness by her use of ellipses and her labeling the story a vision, and by refusing to let Mrs. Hale repeat Mattie's words, Cynthia Wolff, in her introduction to the story, argues, "What it [the frame] gives us, then, is the narrator's *own* explanation for the tragedy he has inferred—an hypothesis, no more, that is formulated as he stands at the juncture that was so fraught with fear in Edith Wharton's own life. The entire 'story' of Ethan Frome's catastrophe is an elaborate theory concocted during that immensely expanded instant when the teller of our tale is waiting at the threshold" (*EF*, xvi).

Stated more strongly, Wolff argues in her *A Feast of Words* that "the man whom we come to know as the young Ethan Frome is *no more than a figment of the narrator's imagination*" (Wolff 1977, 164; emphasis is Wolff's). He is a dream-vision of the narrator's inner self— his "winterman," what he would become if he stayed in Starkfield too many winters, or the man he might become if the appurtenances of his career, and his adult mobility, were taken from him. Ethan is defined by the narrator in heroic terms but also contradictory ones: he is "the most striking figure in Starkfield" but also "the ruin of a man"; he has a powerful look but is bleak and unapproachable. Heroic, yet unable to break out of his impotence, he chooses passivity and repression and forfeits the maturity of adulthood.

Wolff also maintains that *Frome* is a explication of Wharton's private nightmare as well as that of the narrator. Wharton wrote of her own anxiety when she had to cross the threshold of her mother's house. Inside meant repression, the constraints of a strict society that forbids women to have careers, admit to passion, to seek any life outside the rigid confines of the drawing room. In *Ethan Frome,* Wolff argues, the narrator represents Edith's objective look at that life, and Ethan himself is emblematic of what it is to live that life. As she was writing *Ethan Frome,* Wharton had begun to explore her seminal self. Her current affair with Morton Fullerton plunged her into a part of herself she had not touched before, and the discovery was both ecstatic and frightening. Edith was also, says Wolff, gaining mature insight into her own fears of "muteness, of helplessness, of confinement to those elemental activities of eating and sleeping" (Wolff 1977, 171)— perhaps exacerbated by her own experience with S. Weir Mitchell's rest cure. Above all, Wharton feared the part of herself that longed to retreat from the complex adult world into the trivia of her society. With *Ethan Frome* Wharton fleshes out the nightmare, the vision, and rejects it for the horror it is. The shadow self, the "winterman" she feared to become is banished (Wolff 1977, 183).

Wolff's excellent analysis of the story forces us into an expanded reading that somewhat relieves us of the burden of Ethan's hopelessness: it is easier to see him as merely a vision of what could be than to project his circumstances into a statement on the human condition. But Wolff's argument, too, has its ragged edges—for in contending that the vision occurs at the instant the narrator enters the kitchen, and then connecting this step with Wharton's own fear of thresholds, Wolff discounts the fact that the narrator is already over the threshold *before* he enters the kitchen. In fact, readers are told that we first enter the hall, a "low unlit passage," with a staircase at the end. The only furniture in the hall is a kitchen chair, which Ethan uses as a stool for his lantern. Leaving the outside behind, and the light that guides him, Ethan and the narrator walk further into the house, and into the mind. In a deft attention to detail, Wharton has the hall connected to the kitchen by a kitchen chair, the light of the lantern foreshadowing the light in the kitchen. We enter the story, not, perhaps, in the instant Wolff describes, but by a crafted progression from outside to hall to kitchen—from distance to acquaintanceship to the insightful intimacy that enables the narrator to assimilate and articulate Ethan's meaning.

A READING

5

Characterization

NIGHTMARES OF NEED

When Wharton chose to title her story with her central character's name, she made a strategic decision about the focus of the book and, through her emphasis on his fate, concomitantly revisited several of the moral questions so prevalent in her work: duty versus self-fulfillment; devotion to the social fabric versus rebellion; the possibilities for happiness given the contravening moral forces in the universe. Consequently, Ethan's life, both before and after the sledding accident, makes us ask critical questions about relationships and about ourselves. Cynthia Wolff puts it most succinctly: "In the case of friendship or marriage, what form ought the two people's mutual dependence take? To what extent is a lover or spouse morally obliged to relinquish personal satisfaction or even well-being in order to fulfill the emotional demands of his or her partner; and when, if ever, can those demands be deemed excessive? If one has made a commitment to friend, lover, or husband, under what conditions can that commitment be abrogated? And finally, what role does the past play in our present lives."[1] In short, the ageless issues of duty versus love and of one's ability to deal with the dilemmas and restraints of one's psychological and physical life are at the core of *Ethan Frome*. How Ethan responds to these questions has been the critical departure for all who read the book and has its seeds in Wharton's own situation.

On the surface, Ethan and Edith have little in common. Ethan is painfully poor and could not even buy a train ticket west; Edith was never without money, even to the degree that Teddy always carried a $1,000 bill with him when they were traveling in case Edith saw something that struck her fancy. Ethan lives a life of isolated, stolid silence; Wharton was surrounded by friends. Wharton was blessed with good health; Ethan lives in a world of sickness. Wharton's milieu was Paris, Ethan's Starkfield. But the interiors of their lives have deep-rooted similarities.

We have already noted that *Ethan Frome* was the most personal of Wharton's novels and that she took unusual critical care of it. The narrative frame places the story a little more than 24 years after it happened, and Wharton had been married 25 years when she was writing the story, indicating that she had important psychological ties to her fictional situation. That Wharton decided to use a male persona for the narrator even in this autobiographical tale gives credence to her need for further protection from the pains of Ethan. Perhaps it was her cathartic way of nurturing herself both during the painful period of her life when it was written and afterwards when she had the distance to see and reject its truths.

In the years surrounding 1910, Wharton's relationships with the three most important people in her life—her closest friend, Henry James; her lover, Morton Fullerton; and her husband, Teddy Wharton—were in chaos. Henry James had become dangerously ill and had turned from a reliable, stalwart confidant to a piteously weak and frightened man. She wrote to Morton Fullerton on 19 March 1910 of James's condition:

> I was told to come after luncheon; and when I entered, there lay
> a prone motionless James, with a stony stricken face, who just

turned his tragic eyes toward me—the eyes of a man who has looked on the Medusa! The good nephew slipped out, and I sat down beside the sofa, and for a terrible hour looked into the black depths over which he is hanging—the superimposed "abysses" of all his fiction. I, who have always seen him so serene, so completely the master of his wonderful emotional instrument—who thought of him when I described the man in "The Legend" as so sensitive to human contacts and yet so secure from them; I could hardly believe it was the same James who cried out to me his fear, his despair, his craving for the "cessation of consciousness," and all his unspeakable loneliness and need of comfort, and inability to be comforted! "Not to wake—not to wake"—that was his refrain; "and then one *does* wake, and one looks again into the blackness of life and everything ministers to it—all one reads and sees and hears." (*Letters,* 202)

He clung to her despairingly one moment, begging her not to leave ("Don't go, my child, don't go—think of my awful loneliness"), then would suffer sudden mood shifts and could hardly wait for her to go. Wharton was at a loss as to how to help her old friend, especially since she was having an equally difficult time with Teddy.

Teddy Wharton had always been a dilettante with little to occupy his time other than hunting, polo, and managing Edith's life. Having fought severe depression twice in her own life, Edith was poignantly aware of the symptoms in Teddy but felt equally helpless to cure them. As both R. W. B. Lewis and Cynthia Wolff have noted, Wharton's marriage to Teddy had never been very stable. In her autobiographical reminiscence, "Life and I," Wharton characterizes the marriage as essentially sexless, and Teddy clearly sought his physical pleasures elsewhere, ultimately with a series of mistresses he kept at Edith's expense in Boston while she was in Europe. The relationship was largely a parent-child one, with Teddy first playing the father to a complacent, passive, and depressed "daughter." As her career flourished and she had her own sexual awakening with Fullerton, the couple's roles reversed. Teddy became increasingly dependent and irresponsible. Shortly after writing to Fullerton about James, Wharton also wrote him about Teddy:

But I must always either refrain altogether—make the "gran rifiu-to"—or else do what I do with my might. I said I would do this thing, and *I must*. Besides, the situation being what it is, what, *practically*, do you mean by your advice? The Whartons adroitly refuse to recognize the strain I am under, and the impossibility, for a person with nerves strung like mine, to go on leading indef-initely the life I am now leading. They say: "The responsibility rests with his wife—we merely reserve the right to criticize." *He* has only one thought—to be with me all day, every day. If I try to escape, he will follow; if I protest, and say I want to be left alone, they will say that I deserted him when he was ill. The Drs all tell me that as yet compulsory seclusion is impossible, and that practi-cally he may do what he pleases!—And if you knew, if you knew, what the days are, what the hours are, what our talks are, inter-minable repetitions of the same weary round of inanities and puerilities; and all with the knowledge definitely before me, put there by all the Drs, that what is killing me is doing him no good! What, in these conditions, do you advise? Walter Berry wants me to ask for a separation—but that seems to me to have become impossible *now*. (*Letters*, 215)

The separation Berry suggested ultimately became a divorce, but not until after three more years of excruciating vacillation. During those years Teddy was committed to a Swiss sanitarium and treated for depression, then went on a world tour in 1910 in search of diversion. Edith began to contemplate divorce, though all of the social mores of "Old New York" prohibited such an action. Equally prohibitive were her own moral strictures, for she felt an over-whelming sense of guilt about the failure of the marriage. Edith con-tinued to hope, however, and in 1911 returned with Teddy to The Mount, only to find him by now physically well but increasingly psychologically unstable. They had wrenching conversations and arguments, resulting in Edith's suggestion that they live apart. Finally, in 1913, the arrangements were settled. Teddy agreed to repay Edith the $50,000 he had embezzled from her in 1919 to buy a house for his mistress, and the divorce was granted in April. It had been long in the coming, and the despair that motivated it was refracted in art through *Ethan*.

Edith, then, was caught between two weak and clinging men, Teddy and Henry James, both of whom she had loved and continued to care for. The situation with Fullerton was ironically converse. Rather than clinging but attentive like Teddy, or desperately lonely like James, Fullerton was beginning to withdraw. Wharton had begun seeing Fullerton socially in 1907, and by 1908 the relationship had deepened into a passionate affair. In 1909 they spent a memorable night together in London (captured by Edith in her erotic poem "Terminus") and later a delirious summer month together. Wharton's letters leave little doubt that Fullerton opened new worlds of feelings for her and gave her a brief sense of what life could be and what her life had been.

The diary she kept during this time records the ecstasy of a woman whose physical and emotional life had lain dormant for decades. The diary spans the period between 29 October 1907 and 12 June 1908. Its entries are sporadic, and the wording, as one might expect, is awkward. Nonetheless, it records, with some of the ironic detachment acquired in middle age, the revisiting of the emotional intensity usually experienced in adolescence. The fact that Edith was 45 when these feelings surfaced gave them passion and poignancy. But Fullerton was neither reliable nor worthy of such feelings. He had been a protégé of Henry James, had had a brilliant college career but had followed that with a nondistinguished career in journalism. His personal life was equally checkered. He briefly married a French actress but continued his amorous adventures with both men and women. To his credit, several of these affairs were of relatively long duration and seemed to follow a pattern. Cynthia Wolff notes, "His wooing and love-making was [sic] invariably given a lofty tone by his lavish literary inclination, and he wrote sensitive letters to the woman with whom he was involved (these letters occasionally got him into trouble later); his affairs, even when they were most sincerely passionate, seldom lasted longer than three years (Fullerton never made the mistake of confusing a love affair with the preliminaries to marriage, and an eventual termination was implicit in the inception); finally, miracle of miracles, he almost always remained on exceptionally good terms with his former mistresses" (Wolff 1977, 145).

As much as she might have wished to the contrary, Wharton was not to be an exception. Having lived in a hellish marriage and then having experienced an all-consuming love, Wharton knew what a good marriage could be and longed for it. Fullerton was not capable of such depth and remained emotionally, if not physically, aloof. Wharton realized her poverty but had little choice but to accept what was given to her. She vacillated between love and fury, between ecstacy and hurt:

> I said once that my life was better before I knew you. That is not so, for it is good to have lived once *in the round,* for ever so short a time. But my life *is* harder now because of those few months last summer, when I had my one glimpse of what a good camaraderie might be—the kind of thing that some women have at least for a few years! Before I knew you I had grown so impersonal, so accustomed to be my own only comrade, that even what I am going through now would have touched me less. When one is a lonely-hearted & remembering creature, as I am, it is a misfortune to love too late, & as completely as I have loved you. Everything else grows so ghostly afterward. (*Letters,* 216)

After a three-year affair, they did part amicably in 1910. While Fullerton, as always, remained relatively unscathed, Wharton was deeply hurt. She writes to him that year:

> You have made me very unhappy, & that at this moment I have almost the right to ask to be spared!
>
> Everything ahead of me is so dark, Dear, save what you are to me, & what I might be to you. *That* is little enough, heaven knows, for the reasons we know: the fact of all I lack, of all I perhaps never had! But I could be the helpful comrade who walked beside you for a stretch & helped carry your load. And now suddenly you tell me that no one can help you carry it; et il me semble que je m'enfonce seule dans la nuit—
>
> But the last word of all, Dear, is that, whatever you wish, I shall understand; I shall even understand your not understanding—because, as you wrote me once, long ago, in the very beginning: "I love you so much, Dear, that I want only what you want." (*Letters,* 219)

By October of that same year her letters to him, while still revealing their deep connection, have the tone of a mentor, not a lover: "This letter might sound 'priggish' to any one who didn't know me: but you do, & I am not afraid! I want to see your admirable intelligence directing a will as strong as it is fine, with a definite plan of life worked out, & a definite goal aimed at; & I *shall* see it, my Dear, & shall rejoice if I have had ever so small a share in the doing!" (*Letters*, 224).

It is in this atmosphere, then, that Ethan was born. A disconsolate friend, a mentally ill husband, and a distant lover were Wharton's sources of inspiration and an admitted drain on her resilience. She wrote to her friend Elizabeth Lodge on 20 June 1910, "I am hard at work on a short novel which I have taken up since Teddy went to Switzerland, & I hope to have time to get well started while I am here alone. It has been impossible to work except spasmodically these last months, & more & more I find that Salvation is there, & there only" (*Letters*, 217–18).

Cynthia Wolff offers this observation:

> The situation defies conventional explanation. Wharton was not caught in a romantic triangle, torn between her duty to Teddy and love for Fullerton. Instead, husband and lover were in some sense grotesque mirror-images of love deformed: Teddy had insatiable needs, but no trace of normal sexual appetites; Fullerton was the very embodiment of passion, but utterly without any desire for affiliation and thus unwilling to allow his own happiness to depend on Edith Wharton's love. Even to demand what anyone has the right to ask of a lover, then, Edith Wharton risked the unacceptable possibility of appearing to be a burden to him even as Teddy (and for that matter, Henry James as well) had become to her. (Wolff 1987, 236)

It is little wonder that the artistic refraction became a tale of woe.

Ethan's own story, fundamentally, is a simple one. Born and raised in Starkfield on an isolated farm, he briefly escapes to take a year's course at a technological college at Worcester. While there he studies physics, becomes friendly with a professor, and possibly has dreams of becoming an engineer. His father's death and the family's subsequent poverty end his schooling, and he returns home to support his invalid mother. When he can no longer care for farm and parent, his cousin, Zeena Pierce, comes to help nurse his mother. His mother dies in the winter, and, terrified by the silence that will be in the house if he is alone, Ethan marries Zeena. The illness of Ethan's mother is reborn in the sickness of his wife.

Ethan's life continues in placid desolation until the arrival of Zeena's impoverished relative, Mattie Silver. Mattie has lost her parents to death after her father's bankruptcy and is bereft of both means and family until Zeena takes her in to help with the housework. Mattie is everything Zeena is not: bright, healthy, happy, and inefficient. Most important, she gives Ethan a glimpse of happiness. Ethan pursues Mattie, but only in his mind, until Zeena, in her ever-constant search for a new medicine and a new doctor, leaves them alone for one night. In the central scene of the novel, Mattie establishes a hearth for Ethan, fixing him a family dinner and using Zeena's prized pickle-dish though she had been warned not to touch it. The dish is broken. When she returns, Zeena discovers the betrayal and solidifies her determination to have Mattie leave. The idea of separation is intolerable to both Mattie and Ethan, and, on the day of her departure, they make a suicide pact to crash their sled into a tree. The accident brings maiming instead of death. When the narrator sees Ethan, Mattie, and Zeena in their home some 20 years later, Mattie is a hopeless, quarrelsome invalid, Zeena is caring for her, and Ethan has a distinct limp. They are imprisoned in an endless nightmare of need.

ETHAN

Readers have long debated about the moral of such a story and about the personality of a man who could resign himself to death-in-life. Critics have accused Wharton of lacking the vocabulary for happiness, and Ethan's life would give credence to the charge. Certainly his life is so despairing, and his future so bleak, that readers are often forced to defend against empathy, to shield themselves from the possibility that life could offer such hopelessness. If one is to engage the novel, however, one must look beneath Ethan's situation to understand what contributory factors, if any, are inherent in Ethan's own personality.

To attribute Ethan's circumstances to fate, to vicious gods who play with him for sport, is to assimilate despair to a degree that few are willing to accept. Under such a plan, Ethan becomes a pawn in a malignant, deterministic universe where all positive endeavors seem futile. It is Jude Fawley's world in Thomas Hardy's *Jude the Obscure,* but it is a vision that Wharton's story refuses to fully embrace. A comparison of Ethan's world with his fictional predecessor's can, however, sharpen our understanding of Ethan.

Though Hardy's novel is more complex, and more rooted in the social mores of its time, Ethan and Jude do share a welter of despair. Jude's life, like Ethan's, is a series of attempts to better himself, only to be frustrated at every turn. As a young boy, Jude longs to go to Christminister to earn a degree but has to help his aunt in her bakery. Jude meets Arabella Dunn and is tricked into marrying her out of loneliness and sexual attraction. Now locked in a marriage even though Arabella has since left him, Jude meets Sue Bridehead, the woman he is to love until his death, and the woman he should have married. He tries again to be admitted to the university but gives up his dream after receiving a rejection to his one inquiry about matriculation. Jude and Sue do eventually have a family but never marry. After a series of horrendous tragedies—Jude is forced to leave his work because of his relationship with Sue; one of Jude's children kills his other two and then himself; Sue has a stillborn child, sees all the deaths as God's retribution, and masochistically marries a man she despises—Jude finally, and mercifully, takes a suicidal walk in the cold rain and dies of consumption, cursing the day he was born.

The universe does indeed seem pitted against Jude, as it might against Ethan. Both give up scholarly ambitions to help impoverished mother figures; both are imprisoned in marriages that occur out of fear of loneliness and in desperation; both have coincidence weighed against them (Jude countless times, Ethan with the inopportune breaking of the dish); both meet other women who could have, had the timing been different, made them happy; and both see all of their ambitions destroyed. In Hardy's story the relationship between Sue and Jude has much more depth and duration than the brief courtship of Ethan and Mattie, but when one looks at the lives of the two men and the possibilities for happiness open to each, one cannot discount that Wharton and Hardy share an imagination of disaster that leaves little consolation.

Hardy's world view, however, is bleaker than Wharton's. Jude fights with everything that is in him to break the cycle, to fulfill the yearning to learn that he seems to have had since birth. None of his actions offer any relief. In fact, like Sisyphus, Jude's best intentions become consistent avenues for new pain. No matter how hard he struggles, the forces aligned against him are too great, and failure is determined for him—a fate Jude shares with all the heroes of Hardy's major novels: Tess of the d'Urbervilles, the Mayor of Casterbridge, and Clym Yeobright in *The Return of the Native*. Wharton, in contrast, does not leave us without hope in *Ethan Frome*. The narrator is there to offer alternative possibilities, and Ethan does not struggle against his fate to the degree that we credit him with such determination and strength that no possible solutions are left for him or ourselves.

Sinister fate, then, does not control Ethan. But if not the gods, what? Some critics have argued environment. Edwin Bjorkman sees the novel as a social commentary on life in the bleak villages of New England. He argues that love would not have saved Ethan and that the farm would be the same unproductive place even if he had been able to marry Mattie.[2] And truly, poverty does control much of Ethan's life. Though it is bankruptcy that brings Mattie to Ethan, that is the only benefit he ever receives from lack of money. Poverty makes him give up his education, serves as Zeena's excuse for asking Mattie to leave, and serves as his excuse for not leaving with Mattie. Most important, it has filled his time with enervating labor that leaves him little strength at the end of the day. The farm is a sparse one: "Starved apple-trees writhing over a hillside among outcroppings of slate" (*EF*, 15) seem to epitomize it, and Ethan works long hours to scrape a living from harvesting the trees on the land and raising some animals. Zeena's medical bills are a continual drain. The townspeople are no resource. Andrew Hale, whom Ethan briefly hopes to go to for a cash advance, to a lesser degree shares Ethan's problems: "His scrupulously clean shirt was always fastened by a small diamond stud. This display of opulence was misleading, for though he did a fairly good business it was known that his easygoing habits and the demands of his large family frequently kept him what Starkfield called 'behind'" (*EF*, 55).

For a novel written in the opulence of Paris, Edith Wharton does an excellent job of imagining the debilitating world of poverty. Cynthia Wolff calls it an insidious environment (Wolff 1977, 168), and Alfred Kazin notes that it is a matter of record that New England of a century ago seemed socially hopeless and the area rapidly declined in population (Kazin 1987, 135). Harmon Gow also tells us that the smart ones got out of Starkfield.

Elizabeth Ammons goes even further to argue that Wharton expresses much more than vague sympathy or compassion for the poor. Rather, "she expressed anger that any human sensibility should be crushed and ground by poverty into the type of dumb, brute existence of which she (maybe because of her own privileged life) keenly felt the horror" (Ammons, 156). Wharton offers no solutions for this life, and Ethan can never see one. We know only that others have made it out, and they are Ethan's dream people:

> He knew a case of a man over the mountain—a young fellow of about his own age—who had escaped from just such a life of misery by going West with the girl he cared for. His wife had divorced him, and he had married the girl and prospered. Ethan had seen the couple the summer before at Shadd's Falls, where they had come to visit relatives. They had a little girl with fair curls, who wore a gold locket and was dressed like a princess. The deserted wife had not done badly either. Her husband had given her the farm and she had managed to sell it, and with that and the alimony she had started a lunch-room at Bettsbridge and bloomed into activity and importance. Ethan was fired by the thought. Why should he not leave with Mattie the next day, instead of letting her go alone? He would hide his valise under the seat of the sleigh, and Zeena would suspect nothing till she went upstairs for her afternoon nap and found a letter on the bed. (*EF*, 97)

But Ethan's hopes for escape never go beyond the starting of the letter. He opens the drawer to find pen and paper to tell Zeena of his leaving, and here fate mocks him with an ad in the *Bettsbridge Eagle* luring him west, with reduced rates (*EF*, 98). Ethan's dreams are quickly shattered by the harsh reality of his poverty. He is already deeply in debt, and no one will lend him more money. Ethan is also crucially fearful of change and responsibility. He tells himself that he would be willing to risk it if Mattie were not dependent on him, never acknowledging that she could be a contributing partner rather than a drain on his finances. He immediately crumples into despair and inertia: "The inexorable facts closed in on him like prison-warders handcuffing a convict. There was no way out—none. He was a prisoner for life, and now his one ray of light was to be extinguished." (*EF*, 99). Yearning for Mattie Silver, he looks out on the beauty of the night, at "the silver-edged darkness of the woods" and, as he cries, feels "as though all the beauty of the night had been poured out to mock his wretchedness" (*EF*, 99).

The question thus becomes, for critics and readers alike, why doesn't Ethan leave? Money is obviously one definitive reason. But others before Ethan have risked it, and he ultimately refuses to try. Duty to Zeena is another compelling reason. Ethan argues with himself that Zeena would have nowhere to go, but answers his own fears by acknowledging that her people would take her in and that he could eventually contribute to her support. He shores up this logic with the further rationalization that Mattie is even worse off than Zeena, for she has exhausted the charity of her relations. Torn between duty and love, faced with uncertainty and guilt, Ethan opts for negation.

Were the story to end with Ethan's decision to stay, his choice could be deemed a noble one. Unable to desert his wife, he relinquishes happiness in favor of a higher ethic of devotion. But Ethan does not choose to stay. He chooses to escape through death and fails in his attempt. Alfred Kazin argues, in fact, that Ethan is predisposed toward defeat (Kazin 1987, 139). And he is equally predisposed to choose death over life—a fact Wharton continually emphasizes by having Ethan identify with the Fromes who have gone before him. The night he and Mattie are to have dinner together, he passes the graveyard and sees a mocking tombstone that bears his name and has always fascinated him: "SACRED TO THE MEMORY OF ETHAN FROME AND ENDURANCE HIS WIFE, WHO DWELLED TOGETHER IN

PEACE FOR FIFTY YEARS" (*EF,* 59). He wonders if the same epitaph will be written for him.

A wish for Zeena's death is also one of Ethan's fleeting hopes for escape. After walking Mattie home from the dance and still enjoying the feeling of their intimacy, he approaches his house and sees a dead cucumber vine, dangling "from the porch like a crape streamer tied to the door for a death." He has a death vision of Zeena, "her mouth slightly open, her false teeth in a tumbler by the bed" (*EF,* 39). Reality abruptly destroys the dream. Not only is Zeena alive, but she has locked him out of his own home, forcing an unspoken guilty confrontation about his warm feelings for Mattie. The face he has imagined is to appear again just before he aims the sled for the elm. Indeed, it is this recurrence of the Zeena-vision that causes him to swerve and that thwarts his dying. In this guise, then, Zeena becomes more than his wife; she is his morality and his instinct for survival. Loyalty to her is more than a superficial dedication to social mores; in a perverse way it becomes the link to his conscience that renders him unable to act, unable to escape, only able to survive.

That Zeena can have such power over Ethan is one of the most intriguing aspects of the novel. Its source lies deep in Ethan's character and in his heredity. Zeena comes to Ethan when he is in critical need of help, both physically to care for this mother and emotionally to break the deathlike silence that has become his environment. Ethan is by nature "grave and inarticulate," though he is receptive to friendly human intercourse and has a healthy attraction to people. At school in Worcester, he relishes the friendly camaraderie of friends. But when his father dies, he must relinquish these contacts, for the daily drudgery of the farm and the mill keep him too busy for idle conversation with the townspeople. When the day's work is finished, he returns to a mother who has lost her desire to talk, for she hears interior voices who drown out all other discourse. Ethan is surrounded by silence, but he never becomes accustomed to it.

Zeena's arrival, even with her harsh and whining voice, breaks into Ethan's profound isolation, and having been starved for so long, he has lost his ability to discern between relief and relish. When his mother dies, he is terrified by the possibility of a return to his isolation: "After the funeral, when he saw her preparing to go away, he was seized with an unreasoning dread of being left alone on the farm, and before he knew what he was doing he had asked her to stay there with him" (*EF*, 52).

Ethan's fear of once again being alone is understandable, especially given the madness that overcame Ethan's mother when she was faced with such a possibility. Ethan tells us that he always attributed the worst of his mother's troubles to her immobility because of rheumatism. For hours she would sit and watch an empty road that could take her nowhere (*EF*, 16). When Harmon Gow's stage was diverted there, she "picked up" and went to the gate to greet him. When Harmon returns to his old route, she loses this contact with the world and her reason. Faced with such a past and fearful of the present possibility of equal silence, a silence exacerbated by the winter season, Ethan marries. Harmon is later to say of him that he has spent too many winters in Starkfield; certainly this one was the most crucial. Ethan can only muse "that it would not have happened if his mother had died in spring instead of winter" (*EF*, 52).

Ethan's response to isolation is painfully realistic, for we have long known of the profound need for human contact. The myth of the hermaphrodite, for example, is the poetic attempt to come to grips with this element in every individual. In the *Symposium*, Plato tells the story of a mythical being who lived on the earth before there were sexual divisions of men and women. The creature contained both sexes in one body, and because it was thus complete in itself, it had a power that rivaled the gods. Zeus became jealous and split the creature into two sexes. From then on men and women have been forced to seek one another out to overcome their sense of incompleteness.[3] Freud, of course, would have another interpretation for this basic desire, but the conclusion is much the same. We cannot find meaning in life alone but must do so through our relations to other people.

Modern research supports the myth's conclusion and proves Wharton to be unusually perceptive about the effects of silence and isolation on the human spirit. Studies have now determined that the isolation of individuals over periods of days, weeks, months, or years poses major problems. "Experiments with individuals in isolation, deprived of sensory stimulation, suggest that most people cannot take such conditions very long—in many cases not more than a few hours."[4] Ethan is faced with the endless whiteness of New England winters; memories of a mother who aborted all conversation; no one who shares his curiosity or his intellect; a repetitive routine in his work day that blurs the hours of his day and deadens his nights. It is no wonder that he panics and marries.

Marriage, however, does not provide the solace, nor fill the emptiness, as Ethan had hoped. Once again laboratory research has demonstrated what writers have long recorded: when people see too much of each other, they begin to withdraw from each other. Studies done by I. Altman and his colleagues in 1971, for example, of men who were cooped up together for eight days revealed that time spent interacting went from 50 percent of their waking hours during the first four days to 25 percent during the last four days. The findings suggest that people confined together for long periods of time may suffer as much from over exposure to fellow inmates as from a lack of social contact (Penrod, 178).

Ethan, then, is confronted with being denied both the solace of companionship and the healing space of being alone, both of which he, like all of us, psychologically requires. His resulting loneliness is profound. The silence of his mother is assumed by Zeena, and Ethan continually perceives her as taciturn, unapproachable, and threatening. Zeena manipulates Ethan through her silence, and though he is aware of her tactics, he has nothing to respond to, and thus does not. We first see this dynamic between the couple when Ethan begins to notice that Zeena is not happy with Mattie: "Once or twice in the past he had been faintly disquieted by Zenobia's way of letting things happen without seeming to remark them, and then, weeks afterward, in a casual phrase, revealing that she had all along taken her notes and drawn her inferences" (*EF*, 29).

The tension mounts among the three, but again is unspoken: "Zenobia's fault-finding was of the silent kind, but not the less penetrating for that. During the first months Ethan alternately burned with the desire to see Mattie defy her and trembled with fear of the result" (*EF*, 45).

As his feelings for Mattie intensify, so do his foreboding and fear: "At other times her silence seemed deliberately assumed to conceal far-reaching intentions, mysterious conclusions drawn from suspicions and resentments impossible to guess. That supposition was even more disturbing than the other; and it was the one which had come to him the night before, when he had seen her standing in the kitchen door" (*EF,* 54).

Ethan is perceptive enough to realize that he is partially to blame for Zeena's nonresponse. True to his harsh environment, he is by nature stern and reserved, and when he returned to the farm after his father's death, "the silence had deepened about him year by year" (*EF,* 51). Initially he had fought it; sometimes in the long winter evenings he would in desperation entreat his mother to say something—only to be told she is "listening." Recalling his mother's disquieting taciturnity and knowing of several other women who had "turned queer" because of isolation, he is increasingly disturbed by Zeena's silence. When questioned by Ethan, Zeena responds that she is silent because Ethan "never listens" (*EF,* 54) (nor, we suspect, says anything back). Ethan admits to the truth of his stoicism but rationalizes that whenever Zeena does talk, it is only to complain: "The charge was not wholly unfounded. When she spoke it was only to complain, and to complain of things not in his power to remedy; and to check a tendency to impatient retort he had first formed the habit of not listening to her, and finally of thinking of other things while she talked" (*EF,* 54).

Zeena's illness, then, is linked with Ethan's and Zeena's silence, and they are locked in a dance of noncommunication that leads inevitably to a dance of anger. The anger erupts during a discussion of Zeena's sickness and her demand that he hire someone else to help her with the housework. The fight is over money—but really over Mattie. Wharton tells us that it is the "first scene of open anger between the couple in their sad seven years together" (*EF,* 83). It is the only time that Ethan and Zeena ever overtly own the battleground that is their marriage. All of the central issues come forward: Zeena tells Ethan that she needs another hired girl, threatening once again to drain all of Ethan's resources. When Ethan protests that he is unable to pay for two people, Zeena counters with relentless logic that of course they can keep only one; Mattie must go. Ethan draws on family ties; Zeena counters that Mattie is *her* family, she has done her share, and Mattie is someone else's responsibility now. Ethan does not even have a familial sense of duty to reply on. He finds that he is no match for his wife. Confronted with her hard attitude and inexorable face, Ethan is controlled by an impotence that comes from deep within him, and he is overwhelmed by a "despairing sense of his helplessness."

The next sentence in the scene is critical: "You ain't going to do it, Zeena?" (*EF*, 86). The plaintive question mark tells us of Ethan's fate. How different his life would have been had his tone been an explanation point of determined resolve. Instead of taking over his life, he relinquishes it to his wife, and she is a master of such psychological warfare. With a calm supported by cold cruelty, she counters his brief impassioned plea and thrusts at the vulnerability created by his guilt over his feelings for Mattie. Zeena implies that people have already been talking about the household triangle. Ethan is quickly vanquished: "His wife's retort was like a knife-cut across the sinews and he felt suddenly weak and powerless" (*EF*, 87). Ethan now loathes his wife with the hatred of the vanquished for the conqueror and, admittedly, with the hatred of the coward for the strong. Zeena takes to her bed, and Ethan meekly returns downstairs to Mattie but not without silently registering the immense hate he feels for his spouse: "Ethan looked at her with loathing. She was no longer the listless creature who had lived at his side in a state of sullen self-absorption, but a mysterious alien presence, an evil energy secreted from the long years of silent brooding. It was the sense of his helplessness that sharpened his antipathy. There had never been anything in her that one could appeal to; but as long as he could ignore and command he had remained indifferent. Now she had mastered him and he abhorred her" (*EF*, 87).

The tragedy of the scene just witnessed is almost beyond empathy. Ethan is the sole breadwinner in the house, yet he cannot even conceive of asserting his right to equality: "there were no means by which he could compel her to keep the girl under her roof." That it is his roof, too, that common decency would justify supporting Mattie until she could find an alternative does not come to Ethan. Instead he passes his responsibility on to Zeena and blames her for his failure: "She had taken everything else from him; and now she meant to take the one thing that made up for all the others" (*EF*, 88). His lameness 20 years later is a physical manifestation of the spiritual weakness Ethan nurtured since his youth.

While admitting that Ethan's ineffectualness is both vexing and embarrassing, some critics have been more charitable to Ethan. David Eggenschwiler argues that Ethan's helplessness has its source in some admirable traits. Ethan's refusal to fight with Zeena comes from a squeamishness about such degrading confrontations; Ethan refuses to stoop to her level to conquer. His sensibilities "are a moral and psychological advantage: they exist because he is an intelligent, gentle man." Further, his pride has protected him for years against Zeena's attacks, and his complacency has most likely been an effective weapon against her. He, from a place of moral superiority, refuses to fight. Unchecked, Zeena's willfulness and domination grow. The arrangement is a workable one as long as Ethan can be satisfied with this sense of superiority, and as long as Zeena never goes for the kill. But when Ethan needs something beyond unexamined spiritual satisfaction, he finds that he no longer has the strength to fight and that the enemy has, over the years, become too strong for him.[5] Unconscious moral superiority, however, offers little solace, and in Wharton's world the meek do not inherit the earth, or the hereafter.

Unable, then, to respond to anger or directly confront vindictiveness, Ethan rages immobilized. He fares no better when he tries to express positive feelings. His deepening relationship with Mattie is also a study in noncommunication. Initially, Ethan can talk to Mattie; in fact, she is the object of his greatest release. He can share his awe for the beauty of his surroundings, educate her about the heavens, and relieve himself of emotions that had hitherto been bottled up as a "silent ache." Such communication is new to Ethan, and it is a heady experience. He falls deeply in love, and now the silence he realizes is a "silent joy" of shared and understood expressions. Most of Ethan's courtship of Mattie revolves around such nonverbal experiences. He recalls, for example, one of his happy times with her, when, at the church picnic in the spring, he finds her locket: "That was all; but all their intercourse had been made up of just such inarticulate flashes, when they seemed to come suddenly upon happiness as if they had surprised a butterfly in the winter woods" (*EF,* 113).

Unable to speak, neither is Ethan able to write. He finds a brief note from Mattie, telling him not to trouble, a plea impossible to honor. In response, he attempts to write to Zeena to tell her he is leaving but crumples up the note. It is this frustrated attempt at communication, however, that does provide a catalyst to break the silence between the two lovers. As Ethan takes Mattie to the train station, he rides in dreary silence, fantasizing about the past and what might have been. They spend much of the ride not speaking—or when they do talk, it is in simple sentences about the logistics of the future, which say nothing about the emotional death before them. They exchange silences in a tense dance that Wharton is so masterful at creating, until Ethan can stand it no longer and bursts out his frustration: "if I could ha' gone with you now, I'd ha' done it—" (*EF,* 115).

Mattie shows him his crumpled letter but first answers his plea for confirmation with silence—then obliquely lets him know of her own love. The scene continues with a volley of silences, Ethan breaking them by saying that there is nothing he can do, Mattie entreating him to write, and Ethan recognizing the poverty of that. Ethan voices his fear that Mattie will marry, and the logical progression from silence to death is made:

> "I don't know how it is you make me feel, Matt. I'd a'most rather
> have you dead than that!"
> "Oh, I wish I was, I wish I was!" she sobbed.
> The sound of her weeping shook him out of his dark anger,
> and he felt ashamed. (*EF,* 117)

As Ethan and Mattie rehearse their death ride, Wharton continues to emphasize the silence that is theirs. Just as Ethan's inarticulateness is made more poignant by his sensitivity to the world around him, so now is every sound of life intensified against the silence they share. Another sled goes by in a "joyous flutter of bells"; as they draw near the village, they hear the fun of children sledding. Caught up in the activity of the moment, and then his reflections on opportunities lost, Ethan suggests that they too take a quick ride. For a brief moment they both become children again, Mattie enthralled with Ethan's adolescent bravado, Ethan exhilarated by Mattie's frightened dependence.

The ecstasy is brief, the noise and laughter vanish, and the agony begins. The silence returns for the "starless dusk," broken only by the knelling of the church clock telling them they must leave. Faced with parting, Ethan can only speculate immobility: "what's the good of either of us going anywheres without the other one now?" (*EF*, 121). Mattie responds frantically with a plea for a suicide pact, the request coming from the fearful depths within her that are full of her vision of the impending loneliness, isolation, and waste that lie ahead of her.

Ethan at first is appalled at Mattie's suggestion, and Wharton deliberately only outlines what allows him to acquiesce. Just as "some erratic impulse" (*EF*, 118) had prompted Ethan to suggest the first trip down the hill, so now does Mattie seem like "the embodied instrument of fate" (*EF*, 122)—but it is fate stimulated by Mattie's pleas that a strange girl will soon be sleeping in her bed, and Ethan's own vision of endless nights sleeping with a woman he despises:

> She tightened her fierce hold about his neck. Her face lay close to his face.
>
> "Ethan, where'll I go if I leave you? I don't know how to get along alone. You said so yourself just now. Nobody but you was ever good to me. And there'll be that strange girl in the house . . . and she'll sleep in my bed, where I used to lay nights and listen to hear you come up the stairs . . ."
>
> The words were like fragments torn from his heart. With them came the hated vision of the house he was going back to—of the stairs he would have to go up every night, of the woman who would wait for him there. And the sweetness of Mattie's avowal, the wild wonder of knowing at last that all that had happened to him had happened to her too, made the other vision more abhorrent, the other life more intolerable to return to. (*EF*, 121–22)

Ethan tries to escape once again into fantasy. He strokes her hair and kisses her, "and they seemed to be by the pond together in the burning

August sun" (*EF,* 122). But reality, in the form of cold tearful cheeks, intrudes. The spruces surround them in blackness and silence and look like coffins. Instead of fantasizing of hot summer months, Ethan's imagination takes him to death.

The scene that follows, the ride down the hill, has been much debated by critics trying to determine both Ethan's and Wharton's motives. In their trial run, Ethan leads Mattie to the sled and sits behind her, protectively. He boasts of his skill, even though he has to strain to see down the slope. The ride is gleefully successful. On the second coast, Ethan insists on sitting in front. Mattie protests that he cannot steer from there, and Ethan replies that "we'll follow the track." Ethan subconsciously or deliberately leaves his fate to fate. When Mattie continues to protest, Ethan stammers that "I want to feel you holding me." Kenneth Bernard in "Imagery and Symbolism in *Ethan Frome*" argues that Ethan is a weak man and wants to die being cuddled and comforted, with Mattie the protector and shelterer.[6] Cynthia Griffin Wolff agrees with Bernard's interpretation, arguing that Ethan regresses into childhood fantasy and repression in this fateful scene. For Wolff, Ethan is seduced by the vision of Mattie and warmth and summer, drifting back to happier times—feelings he wants to capture and keep, "so that it would sleep there like a seed in winter" (*EF,* 122). Mattie's words have little effect on Ethan, for he is lost in a reverie, having lapsed into the simplicities of infancy (Wolff 1977, 180). The horse cries, and Ethan registers that he must want food, a primal need. Ethan's desire to sit in front, then, is indicative of his passivity, his infantile behavior, his basic impotency, both sexual and psychic.

Jean F. Blackall does not share this view but rather says that Wharton's definition of love as a "sharing of all" would include an ideal of domestic community. Ethan's idea of love therefore is nurture: "he wants to sit ahead of Mattie on the sled so that he, not Mattie, will hit the elm tree first." Ethan here is confirming the values of home, health, and protectiveness.[7]

Blackall supports this stand by noting that the source for Wharton's accident was a disastrous sledding mishap on the Court House Hill in Lenox, Massachusetts. The *Berkshire Evening Eagle* for

12 March 1904 reports that a Hazel Crosby was fatally injured (though not killed instantly) when a sled she was steering hit a tree. The newspaper notes that a young man in the party of five had been steering until the accident, when Ms. Crosby requested to sit in the front and guide the sled for one trip. Permission was reluctantly granted, and in her front position she received the full force of the accident. Wharton knew of the incident because one of the survivors, a Miss Spencer, worked as assistant librarian at the Lenox Library during the time Wharton was associate manager, and Wharton consulted with Spencer while researching her novel.

The question remains, then, was Ethan's decision to sit in front cowardly, infantile, or protective? The answer seems to lie somewhere in that neutral ground of fiction between illusion and reality—like the mist which blurs so much of the story. Ethan clearly has mixed feelings about the death pact. He has only reluctantly agreed to it, and even as they settle into the sled Mattie's warm breath on his neck makes him almost spring to his feet. Then, in a flash he remembers the alternative. Ethan sits in front. Though Mattie protests that he cannot steer from that position, she accepts his reply that he wants to be held. Ethan carefully places the rungs of the sled in the tracks—tracks that he has said will take them to the tree and death.

Clearly, however, Ethan is controlled by forces he does not fully comprehend. He recognizes Mattie's insanity, but she has reached for him from the powerful realms of her own sexual subconscious, touching Ethan in the strongest elements of his own being. She appeals to his nurturing spirit, the only source of his positive sense of self, and then strikes at his more chaotic feelings of physical revulsion for Zeena. Nor is he thinking with any pragmatic clarity. It is difficult to conceive of a more irrational choice for a method to end one's life— but neither Mattie nor Ethan are capable of such logical distance. The tracks he relies on are made by successful sledders and, consequently, must miss the tree. He has to control the sled, therefore, by body movements that in truth leave much to chance, to the tracks, and to fate. With the cruelty of Lear's gods who play with him for sport, Ethan has a brief chance for reprieve as Mattie's breath on his neck jerks him back to reality, but thoughts of Zeena put him back on course. The horse whines as he begins, again bringing to his conscious mind a series of confused images that blur his determination. The images recede, and he repetitively chants "we can fetch it." At the fateful moment, however, the vision reenters: "But suddenly his wife's face, with twisted monstrous lineaments thrust itself between him and his goal, and he made an instinctive movement to brush it aside" (*EF,* 124–25). The sled swerves and breaks the force of the downward ride. Ethan rights it and hits the tree.

Wharton leaves the scene unannotated; it ends with an ellipsis, just as other important parts in the novel have. Are we supposed to believe that Zeena's face appears from his subconsciousness in a last attempt to save him, to remind him of his duty? Or does it appear to remind him of his horror? Does Ethan trust to the tracks because he really does not want to die, or does not want to take responsibility for dying? Did the slight swerve caused by Ethan's instinctive movement break the momentum of the sled just enough to keep the impact from being fatal?

Neither Wharton nor Ethan answers these questions. Wharton chooses deliberate ambiguity, just as much of the novel is centered in uncertainty, described by time schemes that are blurred, a narrator who gets the story years later, and a central character who cannot articulate his feelings or understand them. Her central character responds to visions, dreams, flashes of feelings he cannot order or control, as Wharton must have felt she was doing in her own life. It is a strange sensation for one unused to touching that deep within, and as she does explore these depths in herself, it is no surprise that she felt most at home with *Ethan* of all her novels. Ethan's fate is as indecisive as his visions. We are never told why Mattie and Ethan do not seek death once again. We can only suspect that what was the impulse of the moment, that one brief meeting of the emotions that led Mattie to suggest and Ethan to accept the suicide pact, never returned. He misses the black certainty of death, and the white ecstasy of being able to escape. Instead he is locked in a grey world of neither life nor death but the crippled twisted world of dashed dreams. It is truly a still life of horror.

If Wharton had left Ethan as he was and implied that he was a victim of the gods, the story would be one of relentless, motiveless, and therefore unrewarding tragedy. Indeed, some critics do contend that Ethan's story is so grim, without any redeeming social virtue, that it is ineffective and offers the reader no mitigating catharsis. The bleakness of the denouement does, indeed, bring Wharton as close as she ever comes to writing into fiction Theodore Dreiser's stark naturalistic description of the human condition in *Sister Carrie:*

> Among the forces which sweep and play throughout the universe, untutored man is but a wisp in the wind. Our civilization is still in a middle stage, scarcely beast, in that it is no longer wholly guided by instinct; scarcely human, in that it is not yet wholly guided by reason. On the tiger no responsibility rests. We see him aligned by nature with the forces of life—he is born into this keeping and without thought he is protected. We see man far removed from the lairs of the jungles, his innate instincts dulled by too near an approach to free-will, his free-will not sufficiently developed to replace his instincts and afford him perfect guidance. He is becoming too wise to hearken always to instincts and desires; he is still too weak to always prevail against them. As a beast the forces of life aligned him with them; as a man, he has not yet wholly learned to align himself with the forces. In this intermediate stage he wavers—neither drawn in harmony with nature by his instincts nor yet wisely putting himself into harmony by his own free-will. He is even as a wisp in the wind, moved by every breath of passion, acting now by his will and now by his instincts, erring with one, only to retrieve by the other, falling by one, only to rise by the other—a creature of incalculable variability.[8]

However, Wharton never totally accepts the bleak determinism of Dreiser, never fully subscribes to the inevitableness of tragedy inherent in the naturalistic writers who follow her. Wharton does give Ethan Frome free will in that she affords him avenues to escape that he simply is unable to take advantage of. Jude Fawley struggles—constantly—against his lot and is beaten down by circumstances truly beyond his control. Ethan, on the other hand, retreats before he begins. He has the tragic flaw of reserve—of a fearful unwillingness to risk. He sees his open door and is unable to cross the threshold. He elicits our empathy, and our rejection.

Zeena: Illness Made Powerful

If emotional stasis, moral inertia, and silence are all integral parts of Ethan's character, and thus themes that draw the novel together, then the similar touchstone for Zeena's personality is illness. Zeena first meets Ethan through the illness of his mother, when she comes to his house as a nurse. She brings with her efficiency, a knowledge of medicines, a sense of how to run a household, and, most important for Ethan, she initially brings volubility—breaking the silence that had imprisoned him for so long. When Ethan's mother dies, Ethan transfers his incestuous need to Zeena and asks her to stay.

Ethan soon learns, however, that Zeena's knowledge of medicine comes from her absorption in her own illness. As Ethan ponders moving out of Starkfield and into a town where Zeena would suffer a total loss of identity, Zeena "developed the 'sickliness' which had since made her notable even in a community rich in pathological instances" (*EF*, 53). Zeena, then, takes on illness as an identity and uses it as a weapon.

When we see Zeena, even as a young woman (she is 35 when the story opens), she is old. Her face is drawn and bloodless and creased by "querulous lines from her thin nose to the corners of her mouth" (*EF*, 48). She habitually wears a shawl and wraps her head in yellow flannel when she goes to bed. Often she is described as a crone—a witch in a quilted counterpane:

> Against the dark background of the kitchen she stood up tall and angular, one hand drawing a quilted counterpane to her flat breast, while the other held a lamp. The light, on a level with her chin, drew out of the darkness her puckered throat and the projecting wrist of the hand that clutched the quilt, and deepened fantastically the hollows and prominences of her high-boned face under its ring of crimping-pins. To Ethan, still in the rosy haze of

his hour with Mattie, the sight came with intense precision of the last dream before waking. He felt as if he had never before known what his wife looked like. (*EF,* 40)

Old before her time, bitter beyond her years, Zeena turns to medicine, both as a cure for her perceived ills and as her one connection with both the community and the outside world. Her interactions with neighbors focus on illness, and she is widely perceived to have the honor of being one of the sickest of her community. Zeena goes to visit Mrs. Hale on occasion because Mrs. Hale "in her youth, had done more 'doctoring' than any other woman in Starkfield, and was still a recognized authority on symptoms and treatment" (*EF,* 55). Mrs. Hale, in turn, tells us Zeena has always been sickly and records how illness has given her stature: "I don't know anybody round here's had more sickness than Zeena" (*EF,* 104). Zeena, too, revels in recounting illness, as when she returns from seeing still another doctor and spends the evening meal telling Ethan and Mattie sickening tales of intestinal disturbances among her friends and relatives.

Illness, moreover, provides Zeena with her only real escape from the town. Even in troubled financial times, Zeena can justify traveling to see a doctor, and she avidly seeks one cure after another, primarily, one suspects, to keep in touch with the world and with her own identity. Ethan is oblivious to her condition; she perceives she is wasting away: "I didn't need to have anybody tell me I was losing ground every day. Everybody but you could see it. And everybody in Bettsbridge knows about Dr. Buck. He has his office in Worcester, and comes over once a fortnight to Shadd's Falls and Bettsbridge for consultations. Eliza Spears was wasting away with kidney trouble before she went to him, and now she's up and around, and is singing in the choir" (*EF,* 82). Not only is she wasting away, but she is slowly disintegrating before Ethan's unseeing eyes: " 'All I know is,' she continued, 'I can't go on the way I am much longer. The pains are clear away down to my ankles now, or I'd 'a' walked in to Starkfield on my own feet' " (*EF,* 47).

Searching for doctors to define her, Zeena also uses her illness as a way to keep current. Her reading matter primarily consists of medicine labels and a book "Kidney Troubles and Their Cure." While Ethan's curiosity takes him toward engineering and recent discourses on biochemistry (borrowed from the narrator; *EF,* 12), Zeena's takes her to electric battery cures and patent medicines. In fact, Zeena's mail is almost exclusively from such vendors (*EF,* 4). If Zeena is to survive, each of the remedies must fail. Zeena never learns to use the electric battery; a new powder must always be in the offing.

Zeena's need for illness and medicines to afford her a viable identity and an antidote to her isolation is certainly clinically and historically accurate. In circumstances of deep isolation, people tend to cope by reducing their expectations or by turning to escapes such as drugs or alcohol. Ethan reduces his expectations; Zeena takes to tonics. Had she been wealthy, she probably would have turned to a rest cure or a water spa. Lacking money, Zeena relies on cheaper powders to afford her the escape she needs. Regularly at bedtime Zeena measures out "some drops from a medicine bottle on a chair by the bed, and, after swallowing them," turns her head away and begins to breath asthmatically (*EF,* 42). (Wharton is relentless in her descriptions.)

Zeena would have had a wide range of drops to choose from and social sanction for using them. The tonics were common cures—Mrs. Hale undoubtedly knew of their virtues—and were touted to cure almost anything. A turn-of-the-century advertisement for "Brown's Iron Bitters—A True Tonic," for example, claimed, "A certain cure for diseases requiring a complete tonic, indigestion, dyspepsia, intermittent fevers, want of appetite, loss of strength, lack of energy, malaria, and malarial fevers, to remove all symptoms of decay in liver, kidneys and bowels, assisting to healthy action all functions of these great organs of life. Enriches the blood, strengthens the muscles and gives new life to the nerves."[9]

Few could resist such instant cures from the harsh life around them, and many women, like Zeena, did not. The tonics were liberally prescribed by doctors for all forms of illness and especially for cure of "female problems." Lacking any pharmaceutical regulations, prescriptions were frequently refilled at will, and over-the-counter tonics were staples of many homes. Most of the tonics contained liberal amounts of either alcohol or opium, or possibly both. Lydia

Pinkham's Vegetable Compound, one of the most popular of all tonics (Ms. Pinkham began marketing her compound in 1875; the family sold the company in 1968) was 20.6 percent alcohol by volume, or over 40 proof. Pinkham's Compound was largely used to cure female complaints, a serious concern of the times, as a Pinkham ad will testify: "A Fearful Tragedy/A Clergyman of Stratford, Conn,/ Killed by his own wife/Insanity brought on by 16 years of suffering with/Female Complaints the Cause/Lydia E. Pinkham's Vegetable Compound/The Sure Cure for these complaints/would have prevented the Direful Deed."[10] Ministers joined with the doctors to support the patent medicine trade. The Balm of Gilead, for example, was a patent medicine recommended by numbers of "retired clergymen." It was 70 percent alcohol, or 140 proof; few rums of today can make that claim.

Many of these tonics were heavily laced with opium or opium derivatives. Paregoric (camphorated tincture of opium) has long been a mainstay for everything from toothaches to constipation—or the intestinal disorders of Zeena's friends and Eliza Spears's kidney trouble. McMunn's Elixir (denarcotized laudanum prepared in ether) and Dover's powders (ipecac and opium used for night sweats) were common to any druggist. The use of such remedies was slowly becoming recognized as more of a health problem than a cure, and as early as 1872 a study was done by the Massachusetts Board of Health on the use and abuse of opium. The study found that opium, in its various forms, was the primary ingredient of doctor's prescriptions and the base for many patent medicines and that women were the largest users. The author of the report, F. E. Oliver, attributed the disproportionate use by women to the life they led: "Doomed, often, to a life of disappointment, and, it may be, of physical and mental inaction, and in the smaller and more remote towns, not unfrequently, to utter seclusion, deprived of all wholesome social diversions, it is not strange that nervous depression, with all its concomitant evils, should sometimes follow—opium being discreetly selected as the safest and most agreeable remedy."[11] But the hope of relief and escape outweighed for most women the possible side effects—especially when those effects were not widely known, even in Zeena's time.

Moreover, the rise of the temperance movement made any other similar escape unacceptable. Women could justifiably carry on an active social gospel crusade against alcohol, while dosing themselves with Brown-Sequard's or Gross's neuralgia pills, which contained high levels of morphine and alcohol. The Massachusetts State Board analyst in 1904 listed the alcohol content of some popular patent medicines. The list is revealing: Paine's Celery Compound, 21 percent; Thayer's Compound Extract of Sarsaparilla, 21.5 percent; Carter's Physical Extract, 22 percent; Parkers' Tonic "purely vegetable," 41.6 percent. By comparison beer contains from 2 to 8 percent alcohol by volume (Haller and Haller, 275, 279–80, 288, 289). While men were frequenting saloons forbidden to their wives, women had a time-honored tradition of exchanging medical remedies and comparing their value, much like modern discussions of fine wines. Undoubtedly, Zeena has carried on many discussions about remedies, without ever acknowledging their hidden worth.

Wharton makes no direct mention of the content of Zeena's tonics, but it is very likely that whatever she regularly takes is both narcotic and alcoholic. Moreover, Wharton had already dealt with the dangers of female medicines and the availability of opiates in her earlier novel *The House of Mirth* (1905). Lily Bart, ultimately finding herself disgraced and doomed to a life of drudgery, dies of an overdose of chloral (a mixture of alcohol and opium). Wharton describes her purchase of the drug in this way:

> Over the counter she caught the eye of the clerk who had waited on her before, and slipped the prescription into his hand. There could be no question about the prescription: it was a copy of one of Mrs. Hatch's, obligingly furnished by that lady's chemist. Lily was confident that the clerk would fill it without hesitation; yet the nervous dread of a refusal, or even of an expression of doubt, communicated itself to her restless hands as she affected to examine the bottles of perfume stacked on the glass case before her.
>
> The clerk had read the prescription without comment; but in the act of handing out the bottle he paused.
>
> "You don't want to increase the dose, you know," he remarked.

Lily's heart contracted. What did he mean by looking at her in that way?

"Of course not," she murmured, holding out her hand.

"That's all right: it's a queer-acting drug. A drop or two more, and off you go—the doctors don't know why."

The dread lest he should question her, or keep the bottle back, choked the murmur of acquiescence in her throat; and when at length she emerged safely from the shop she was almost dizzy with the intensity of her relief. The mere touch of the packet thrilled her tired nerves with the delicious promise of a night of sleep, and in the reaction from her momentary fear she felt as if the first fumes of drowsiness were already stealing over her.[12]

Zeena's exact illness is shrouded in mystery. We know only that she is a morbid hypochondriac and that she gets incrementally worse as Ethan get progressively happier. After the fateful visit to still another doctor that leaves Mattie and Ethan alone, she returns with assurances that "I'm a great deal sicker than you think." "Troubles" have moved to "complications," and tonics should now be supplemented with an operation: "She continued to gaze at him through the twilight with a mien of wan authority, as of one consciously singled out for a great fate. 'I've got complications,' she said. . . . Ethan knew the word for one of exceptional import. Almost everybody in the neighborhood had 'troubles,' frankly localized and specified; but only the chosen had 'complications.' To have them was in itself a distinction, though it was also, in most cases, a death-warrant. People struggled on for years with 'troubles,' but they almost always succumbed to 'complications'" (EF, 81).

Ethan does not know the details of these ailments, nor do we— but we know they have the social sanction of the community, for somebody had told Mrs. Hale about Zeena's trip to Bettsbridge to see the new doctor, and Mrs. Hale in turn tells Ethan that she hopes Zeena will find a cure. Her voice is compassionate, with no hint of censure for Zeena's medical odyssey.

If Zeena uses her illness for connection, for identity, and for social status, she also uses it as a weapon. Wracked by her own pain, both real and imaginary, she transfers her agony to Ethan. Ethan recognizes that Zeena has become increasingly bitter over the years, that "she was a hundred times bitterer and more discontented than when he married her." With deep resentment he sees "the one pleasure left her was to inflict pain on him" (*EF, 96*).

Unfortunately, Zeena's response to her environment is not a unique one. Women in the late nineteenth century, condemned to a life of legal powerlessness, often used illness as a means both to gain control over their environment and to mitigate some of the grueling demands of housework. Enjoying their power, many sick women showed little inclination to get well.

The common terminology for hypochondria and general ill health such as Zeena's was hysteria. In the beginning of the nineteenth century the ailment, primarily ascribed in women, was defined by complaints of depression, nervousness, chronic fatigue, disabling pain, and a tendency for hysterical "fits." These fits, as described by the medical literature of the period, were usually precipitated by sudden shocks to the emotions and were described thus: "It began with pain and tension, most frequently in the 'uterine area.' The sufferer alternately sobbed and laughed violently, complained of palpitations of the heart, clawed her throat as if strangling and at times, abruptly lost the power of hearing and speech. A death-like trance might follow, lasting hours, even days. At other times violent convulsions—sometimes accompanied by hallucinations—seized her body."

During the first half of the century, a diagnosis of hysteria usually required the presence of at least one of these episodes. By the end of the century, however, the definition of the disease had broadened to include almost every known ailment—thus the wide-ranging claims of the tonics. The symptoms could include "loss of sensation in part, half, or all of the body, loss of taste, smell, hearing, or vision; numbness of the skin, inability to swallow, nausea, headaches, pain in the breast, knees, hip, spine or neck, as well as contracture or paralysis of virtually any extremity."[13]

Nor were the symptoms limited to the physical. Doctors saw these women as narcissistic, highly impressionable, egocentric in the extreme. Zeena is emotionally well qualified to be a patient and has solid social company for her behavior. She, like her neighbors, can use her illness as a catalyst to get what she wants. By constantly complaining of illness and its subsequent physical weaknesses, she is able to ask for domestic help without feeling guilty or looking selfish. Indeed, when Mattie is forced to leave, there is no question in Zeena's mind but that she will be replaced by someone capable of helping her with the work. Ethan supports this notion by initially assuming that the new hired girl will be in addition to Mattie, not in place of. Moreover, he has long accepted Zeena's physical disability, first by agreeing to let Mattie come in the first place and then by compensating for her inefficiency:

> Zeena has always been what Starkfield called "sickly," and Frome had to admit that, if she were as ailing as she believed, she needed the help of a stronger arm than the one which lay so lightly in his during the night walks to the farm [Mattie's]. . . . He did his best to supplement her unskilled efforts, getting up earlier than usual to light the kitchen fire, carrying in the wood overnight, and neglecting the mill for the farm that he might help her about the house during the day. He even crept down on Saturday nights to scrub the kitchen floor after the women had gone to bed; and Zeena, one day, had surprised him at the churn and had turned away silently, with one of her queer looks. (*EF*, 27)

By using her illness as an excuse, she can also drain Ethan of his financial resources and thereby keep him dependent on the farm, and her. Ethan knows this but is powerless to counter it. When Zeena announces that she is going to seek still another cure, Ethan winces: "Twice or thrice before she had suddenly packed Ethan's valise and started off to Bettsbridge, or even Springfield, to seek the advice of some new doctor, and her husband had grown to dread these expeditions because of their costs. Zeena always came back laden with expensive remedies, and her last visit to Springfield had been commemorated by her paying twenty dollars for an electric battery of which she had never been able to learn the use" (*EF*, 46).

He compounds his difficulty by lying, telling her that he needs to go to see Mr. Hale to collect a cash payment: "He knew from experience the imprudence of letting Zeena think he was in funds on the eve of one of her therapeutic excursions" (*EF*, 48).

Ethan regrets having given Zeena an opening for spending more money but dismisses his fears with thoughts of being with Mattie and not having to ride with Zeena. Obviously, his motives for not countering Zeena are mixed. Rather than fear her malady for the pathology it is (though he does admit that he fears her "going queer" out of loneliness), he deflects his concern to money. Zeena's fragility does afford the reason for having Mattie in the house. Until Mattie arrived, all of these expenses were a drain on Ethan. With Mattie there, even Zeena's illness momentarily takes a positive turn. She is so totally absorbed, Ethan believes, in her own health that she does not notice his growing enthusiasm for her cousin. Her trips to the doctor afford Ethan time alone with Mattie. But the advantages gained from the illness are brought to an abrupt end when Zeena, looking for her stomach powders, finds the broken pickle-dish.

There is little question, however, that Zeena is well aware of the power struggle around her. The "queer look" she had given Ethan when she catches him doing Mattie's work lets us know she is a strategist. When she is to leave for Starkfield, and just after Ethan has lied to her about getting the payment, she pretends not to hear but she measures out a large draught from her tonic and replies: "It ain't done me a speck of good, but I guess I might as well use it up" (*EF*, 49). In a masterstroke of structured symbolism, Wharton next has her push the empty bottle toward Mattie: "If you can get the taste out of it, it'll do for pickles" (*EF*, 99).

In this battle of physical ills, Zeena is clearly the victor. She manipulates Ethan through guilt into staying with her; he is afraid of leaving a sickly wife "whom his desertion would leave alone and destitute" (*EF*, 105). "Even if she were in better health than she imagined, [she] could never carry such a burden alone" (*EF*, 98). Her constant use of medicine and pilgrimages to doctors leave him drained of resources. He does not even have the money for train tickets for two. More knowledgeable than Ethan, the reader senses throughout the novel that Zeena is capable of taking care of herself. Events prove that she is also more than strong enough to take care of others as well. In fact, Mrs. Hale tells us: " 'Yes, there she's been,' Mrs. Hale continued, 'and Zeena's done for her, and done for Ethan, as good as she could. It was a miracle, considering how sick she was—but she seemed to be raised right up just when the call came to her. Not as she's ever given up doctoring, and she's had sick spells right along; but she's had the strength given her to care for those two for over twenty years, and before the accident came she thought she could't even care for herself'" (*EF*, 131). No longer needing to be sick to survive, Zeena lays down her weapon—but never so far away that she cannot arm herself again with an occasional "sick spell."

Zeena, then, uses her illness to give herself an identity in the community, to escape isolation, and to control those around her. Consumed by her sense of disease, she resents any happiness in others. One critic has noted that Zeena distrusts pleasure in general, in the Calvinistic ascetic belief that you are more likely to enter the Kingdom of Heaven if you deny yourself worldly gratification. Denying it in yourself, you cannot sanction it for anyone else.[14] One recalls H. L. Mencken's definition of Puritanism as the fear that somewhere someone will be happy.

The reader's reaction to Zeena is mixed, as Wharton intended. Ethan did, after all, marry Zeena. And while he admittedly made no emotional commitment to her, having married her out of spontaneous desperation, he has made a legal commitment to support her. Conversely, Zeena's pure meanness, her constant whining, her passive-aggressive manipulation of Ethan, her abuse of Mattie, even her seeming relish of the ugly, make her an extremely unsympathetic character. That Wharton deliberately tilts our sympathy away from her is even manifest in her choice of names for her characters. In the original draft of the novel, Zeena was called "Anna," which comes from the Hebrew word for "grace." The onomatopoetic Zeena is deftly more appropriate.

As she does in so many of her stories, once again Wharton calls upon us to choose between what is socially sanctioned—support of the marriage regardless of its character—or modicum of human happiness in a world overwhelmingly weighed with sadness. Within the plot,

Wharton does not clearly resolve the dilemma, but she does weigh the emotional balance decidedly against Zeena. In fact, Geoffrey Walton has argued that there is an element of caricature in the treatment of her, given that she is the epitome of dyspepsia and uncharitableness.[15]

In an equally convincing argument, Elizabeth Ammons sees Zeena as a witch and interprets the story as a parallel to the fairy tale of Snow White. Zeena's physique is witchlike: shallow complexion, premature aging, high cheek bones, thin drab hair, piercing eyes, a giant nose, sharp chin—all the features nightmares are made of. She is also the older woman who takes in a orphan girl, thus becoming her (wicked) stepmother. Like the witches of old, Zeena is childless, frigid, spectral (the house is described as "having the deadly chill of a vault") and even has the archetypal cat as an accomplice.

Witchlike, she constantly belittles Mattie and tortures Ethan with her whining. She even haunts him: mentioning her name, on the one evening Mattie and Ethan share, "throws a chill between them." Or, when Ethan first enters the kitchen on the same night, he notes: "So strange was the precision with which the incidents of the previous evening were repeating themselves that he half expected, when he heard the key turn, to see his wife before him on the threshold; but the door opened, and Mattie faced him. . . . She stood just as Zeena has stood, a lifted lamp in her hand, against the black background of the kitchen" (*EF,* 60).

At this instance Mattie, too, takes on the black-white coloration of a crone: "She held the light at the same level, and it drew out with the same distinctness her slim young throat and brown wrist no bigger than a child's. Then, striking upward, it threw a lustrous fleck on her lips, edged her eyes with velvet shade, and laid a milky whiteness above the black curves of her brows" (*EF,* 60). Later, as the intimate evening progresses, Ethan asks Mattie to come nearer to him, only to realize "as her young brown head detached itself against the patch-work cushion that habitually framed his wife's gaunt countenance, Ethan had a momentary shock. It was almost as if the other face, the face of the superseded woman, had obliterated that of the intruder" (*EF,* 66).

Even more terrifying, in Wharton's tale there is no miraculous rescue of the maiden. The witch wins, just as the witch before her, Ethan's mother, had won. And not only does the witch win, she multiplies (Ammons, 62ff). Mattie becomes Zeena's double, and they remain locked not in a fairy tale of fantasy, but a nightmare of need. That this was Wharton's most personal of novels becomes most painfully clear here, as her deliberations about what to do with the "slightly queer" Teddy made the nightmarish life of Ethan a personally terrifying prospect for her.

MATTIE: THE MAIMED MAIDEN

If Zeena is the witch figure in Wharton's tale, Mattie is the fairy maiden. Beautiful, youthful, happy, she is everything that Zeena is not. The imagery Ethan associates with her is sexual. As they sit together on the fateful night, the scent of geraniums mingles with Ethan's smoke (*EF*, 67). Their communication takes on an air of loving, established intimacy. He meditates on their possible life together, fantasizing about what could be. Prophetically, however, he says, "This is the night we were to have gone coasting, Matt" (*EF*, 67). After the dish is broken, he assures her he has taken care of it, and her passive gratitude stirs his masculinity, her dependence makes him feel strong. In phallic meditation he muses, "Except when he was steering a big log down the mountain to his mill he had never known such a thrilling sense of mastery" (*EF*, 64). Coupled with this sense of dominance is a romantic dream of secret gardens, hair that smells of woods, romantic glens—all parts of Ethan's fantasy world of Mattie, a fantasy he is impotent to realize: "Ethan felt confusedly that there were many things he ought to think about, but through his tingling veins and tired brain only one sensation throbbed: the warmth of Mattie's shoulder against his. Why had he not kissed her when he held her there?" (*EF*, 43).

Ammons persuasively argues that Ethan does not make love to Mattie because he does not want to "ruin her"—and thereby spoil his fantasy. She must forever stay the young woman—though clearly his dream of her does mature into seeing her as cook and caretaker in his house. Woman as young virgin, woman as nurturer—both visions exclude the sexual, and at Ethan's peril, for when the sexual elements do surface, they gain relentless and devastating control (Ammons, 65).

Mattie, with her sexual connotations for Ethan, represents the life force in the novel—a life force that has until now been virtually unexamined by Ethan. Like the color red associated with her, she is "the lighting of a fire on a cold hearth" (*EF*, 25). Almost naively full of wonder herself, she is Ethan's avenue into the wondering side of himself: "The girl was more than the bright serviceable creature he had thought her. She had eyes to see and ears to hear: he could show her things and tell her things, and taste the bliss of feeling that all he imparted left long reverberations and echoes he could wake at will" (*EF*, 25). She brings joy to Ethan; he is never gay except in her presence.

But her virtues are also the source of her vulnerability, especially to the practical, prosaic Zeena. While Mattie is quick to learn housework, she is "forgetful and dreamy," not prone to take it seriously. She is the playful side of life itself, but in the bleak world of Wharton's vision, play does not balance pain, nor does it equip one for survival. It is with consummate irony, then, that Ethan and Mattie are maimed on a childlike sled ride.

If Mattie brings life to Ethan, so does he bring life to her. He notes that she has radically changed since coming to Starkfield. She arrives a child, "a colourless slip of a thing," having been orphaned by the death of her father and the subsequent death of her mother at the disclosure of her husband's insolvency. Mattie comes to Starkfield able "to trim a hat, make molasses candy, recite 'Curfew shall not ring to-night,' and play 'The Lost Chord' and a pot-pourri from 'Carmen'" (*EF*, 44). While in Starkfield, she learns at least to do some housework and to suppress any bitterness at her fate in deference to the precariousness of her situation. Ethan's evident caring concern for her nurtures her seemingly irrepressible spirit of happiness. Our first glimpse of Mattie, in fact, comes through the young Ethan's eyes as he stares through the window at her while she dances, catching the fire of her partner's passion. Her joy, and her relish in the attentions of another man, force Ethan's jealousy to the surface, and he rages within himself; he wants to horsewhip Denis Eady.

Such violent or decisive acts, however, are not in Ethan's nature. He passively waits his turn. Mattie is offered a ride home but refuses it, hoping for Ethan. Ultimately, Ethan does step out of the shadows, and the two briefly share their joy in each other—but not without the ever-present shadow of Zeena's illness. Mattie has feared that Ethan was not coming back for her because "Zeena wasn't feeling any too good to-day" (*EF*, 34).

Zeena's illness, then, taints everything in the novel. This manipulative agent thwarts Ethan's happiness and infects the spirit of life that is Mattie. Nor is the malignancy of sickness only present in Zeena; it is also the reason for Mattie's being in Starkfield, and her frailty is one source of Ethan's concern for her when she is told to leave. Before moving to the Frome's, Mattie had tried bookkeeping and stenography, but her health broke. (And we are led to believe that, unlike Zeena, she was physically sick.) Long hours of standing in a department store do not help her any, and she comes to Starkfield already debilitated by her past. When Zeena forces her to leave, she realizes she will be destroyed by her future. Ethan asks her where will she go; she replies, " 'I might get something to do over at Stanford.' She faltered, as if knowing that he knew she had no hope" (*EF*, 90).

As Elizabeth Ammons so convincingly demonstrates, Mattie's future is indeed grim: "She can work in a factory and lose her health; she can become a prostitute and lose her self-dignity as well; she can marry a farmer and lose her mind." The research of Anna Garland Spencer, a contemporary of Wharton, demonstrated that many young women who worked during the unmarried years between 14 and 20 did lose their health. She notes what they endured:

> . . . in the canning factories 2,400 rapid and regular motions a day in tin-cutting for the girls employed. . . . In the confectionery business, 3,000 chocolates "dipped" every day at a fever heat of energy. In the cracker-making trade, the girls standing or walking [all day] not six feet from the ovens. . . . In the garment trades the sewing machines speeded to almost incredible limits, the unshad-

ed electric bulbs and the swift motion of the needle giving early
"eye-blur" and nerve strain. . . . In department stores . . . where
five or six hundred girls are employed nineteen to thirty seats may
be provided; but to use even these may cost the girl her position.
(Ammons, 71, 70, 71)

Mattie's fear of factory labor therefore is realistic. Since she
already proved too frail to be a stenographer, even the revitalizing
time in Starkfield would not be sufficient for her to survive such conditions.

The possibility of Mattie becoming a prostitute is too horrifying
for Ethan, or even Wharton, to face:

He dropped back into his seat and hid his face in his hands.
Despair seized him at the thought of her setting out alone to
renew the weary quest for work. In the only place where she was
known she was surrounded by indifference or animosity; and
what chance had she, inexperienced and untrained, among the
million bread-seekers of the cities? There came to back to him
miserable tales he had heard at Worcester, and the faces of girls
whose lives had begun as hopefully as Mattie's. . . . It was not possible to think of such things without a revolt of his whole being.
He sprang up suddenly. (*EF*, 90–91)

Though it does not take a strong leap of imagination to share
Ethan's terror at such a vision, especially given his own sexual connection to Mattie, in fact her physical life on the streets would not have
been severely worse than her life in a factory. The *Summary Report on
the Condition of Women and Child Wage Earners in the United States*
(1916), which deals with the period contemporary with Mattie, found
that prostitution provided economic survival and sometimes even
upward mobility. The report records that the average weekly wage for
1,600 department store employees and factory women was $6.67.
Moreover, the same study revealed that in predominantly female
industries—glass, cotton, silk, and men's ready-to-wear clothing—
"from two-fifths to two-thirds of those women 16 years of age and
over earned less than six dollars in a representative week." Since most

authorities agreed that a working woman who lived alone needed a minimum weekly wage of nine dollars, such jobs clearly offered only a subsistence income.

By contrast, a prostitute could earn in one night what a working woman earned in a week. The hours were shorter—usually from nine in the evening until two in the morning. If the women lived in even an average brothel, the meals were guaranteed, and she was allowed to sleep in the morning and have her afternoons free.[16] Obviously, better hours, better money, and better housing do not make up for the personal degradation involved in such a life, and no one would defend the profession as a viable one for Mattie. But given the alternative working conditions, including the common sexual harassment from employees in the "respectable trades," the temptation for factory hands to sell all of their bodies instead of just pieces of them was great.

The third option open to Mattie, though even less a possibility than the other two, is to continue to do housework and farm labor. But such jobs were difficult to find (note the ease with which Zeena finds a replacement for Mattie), and Mattie is not good at the work. Moreover, Mattie and Ethan both know the effects of physical isolation or social isolation because of class. Ethan's own mother had become "queer," and Zeena's silence is broken only by neurotic complaining. In her French draft of the novel, Wharton interpolates that Mattie "exemplified all the dull anguish of the long line of women who, for two hundred years, had been buffeted by life and who had eaten out their hearts in the constricted and gloomy existence of the American countryside" (Ammons, 77). The final version of the novel is more subtle, but no less devastating.

Mattie, then, is trapped by an economic system that leaves her no visible alternatives. Her chances for economic success are thwarted by her father's death and her lack of education, even as Ethan's hopes for an education that would have freed him are thwarted by his father's death and mother's illness. Without financial backing, she is severely handicapped in the marriage market. She has had the standard education for a middle-class girl of her time, but there is no market for poor candy makers who can play potpourris from *Carmen*.

Financially destitute, ill-trained for work or life; destined to lose rapidly her only marketable commodity, her youth; faced with grueling labor, a life on the streets, or destructive isolation; and in love with a man whose own chains are overwhelming to him, is it any wonder that it is Mattie who suggests the sled ride? Like her mother before her, confronted with both emotional and financial poverty, she chooses death.

The final sled ride, with all its possibilities for release, is a macabre comment on the human condition. Symbolically, Mattie and Ethan have chosen "coasting" as a vehicle for death, just as Ethan has coasted through his life. Mattie, as a representative of life who now wants death, becomes the catalyst for fate. Zombielike Ethan follows her hysteria. Mattie loses to illness, to death-in-life, to Zeena. Ethan, almost pitiful in his naïveté, had seen Mattie as the future, but now Zeena lies ahead. Making sure that Ethan does not make the same mistake again—to hope for happiness and fulfillment in a universe designed to thwart such desires—Wharton makes the transformation complete. Mattie becomes Zeena; Zeena rises phoenixlike, reborn by the possibility of emasculating Ethan forever and keeping Mattie hopelessly dependent, of being the powerful witch she has aspired to be. Joy is turned to endurance, like the name on the tombstone in the Frome graveyard: "SACRED TO THE MEMORY OF ETHAN FROME AND ENDURANCE HIS WIFE, WHO DWELLED TOGETHER IN PEACE FOR FIFTY YEARS" (*EF*, 59).

6

Setting and Symbolism

Whether Ethan's story is a vision, a tangled web of different stories, or both, Harmon Gow believes the source of Ethan's predicament is that "he's been in Starkfield too many winters." In her own comments on the novel, Wharton notes that she believed most New England fiction, and especially Sarah Orne Jewett's, bore little resemblance to "the harsh and beautiful land" as she had seen it. The abundant description "of sweet-fern, asters and mountain-laurel, and the conscientious reproduction of the vernacular, left [her] with the feeling that the outcropping granite" had been overlooked (*EF*, xix). Certainly the setting of the story has a rock-hard atmosphere, but it is also an ironic metaphor for the balancing contrasts that permeate the story.

The narrator tells us early on that he is struck by the contrast between the crispness of the climate and the deadness of the community: "Day by day, after the December snows were over, a blazing blue sky poured down torrents of light and air on the white landscape, which gave them back an intense glitter. One would have supposed that such an atmosphere must quicken the emotions as well as the blood; but it seemed to produce no change except that of retarding still more the sluggish pulse of Starkfield" (*EF*, 7).

Crystal clearness is followed by long stretches of sunless cold, and the storms of February only lead to the biting winds of March. With climate so formidable, it is easy to capitulate to routine and to be hypnotized into a "grim satisfaction in the life." When survival against the cold is all-consuming, it is difficult to nurture intimacy. It is no coincidence that Ethan's maiming takes place in February, that the vehicle is a sled, that the occasion for the narrator's glimpse into Ethan's experience is a blinding snowstorm. And if Jewett's restful summer evenings and warm breezes can lull one into complacency, so can the raging storms so deaden the senses that monotony goes unnoticed.

Harmon Gow does not say that Ethan has been in Starkfield too long, but that he has been there "too many winters." In his own taciturn way, Gow is expressing one of the crucial aspects of place in the novel. Everywhere there is snow. The train that the narrator is supposed to take to the plant is blocked by a freight that got stuck in a drift. His first glimpse of Ethan's house is of a lonely New England farmhouse "huddled against the white immensities of land and sky" (*EF*, 15); the boundaries of the fields surrounding it are lost under the drifts. As they travel toward the station, the landscape is "chaotically tossed" by gales blowing the new snow. When he returns to have Ethan carry him home, "the snow began to fall straight and steady from a sky without wind, in a soft universal diffusion more confusing than the gusts and eddies of the morning" (*EF*, 17). The narrator gets out of the sleigh and leads the horse through the snow until they come to Ethan's house, all winded by the "bitter cold and the heavy walking." Even when we return in a flashback to the young Ethan, the chapter opens with "the village lay under two feet of snow" (*EF*, 20).

We enter Ethan's history in medias res, just as we have earlier entered the narrator's life when he is middle-aged and passing through. Because of the imagination of the narrator, and because he has both a discerning eye and a love of nature, we know more, or at least we think we know more, of Ethan's early environment than if we had to rely on any of Starkfield's inhabitants to tell us the story directly. We know that even when times were better, some things remained the same—the ubiquitous snow of the frame story, for example. In the flashback young Ethan is seen looking in the church, standing outside in a "complete absence of atmosphere," with "the white earth under his feet and the metallic dome overhead" (*EF*, 21). Contrasting with the frigidity of Ethan's external world is the scene inside, a room "seething in the midst of heat" (*EF*, 22), a room that contains Mattie, the girl who has brought heat into his life.

The snowy chill of Starkfield, the blistery winter of the interior story, is the bleak backdrop for the entangled relationships and serves as a foreshadowing of tragedy. When Mattie leaves the church with Ethan, she relinquishes the warmth of the dance to walk back toward their house, down a hemlock-shaded lane, passing a gloomy sawmill, moving through "grey and lonely" country. A farmhouse stands "mute and cold as a grave-stone." The frozen snow crackles under their feet. Unremittingly, the snow, ice, and sleet twist Ethan's plans and ultimately become the instrument of his destruction. His mare slips on ice and delays his trip to the village to buy glue; then the logs are coated with sleet, making them doubly difficult to load, and Ethan must give up the trip altogether. After dinner he does get to the village and hopes to beat Zeena home, only to have the sleet and rain delay him again. When Ethan must take Mattie to the train, the setting mirrors his emotions. Instead of taking the direct route to Starkfield, Ethan goes up Bettsbridge road toward Shadow Pond. It is a fantasy trip, and derisively the scenery mocks his vision: "The lane passed into a pine-wood with boles reddening in the afternoon sun and delicate blue shadows on the snow. As they entered it the breeze fell and a warm stillness seemed to drop from the branches with the dropping needles. Here the snow was so pure that the tiny tracks of wood animals had left on it intricate lace-like patterns, and the bluish cones caught in its surface stood out like ornaments of bronze" (*EF*, 112). But the setting is infused with the "same dull melancholy that Ethan felt in his heart." All warmth is in the past, a memory of a single summer afternoon where Ethan had joined Mattie at a picnic on this spot and had found her lost locket. Now there is only a "fallen tree-trunk half submerged in snow" (*EF*, 113).

Mattie's and Ethan's brief stop at Shadow Pond en route to their separation is a dream-vision—one that Ethan is reluctant to relinquish.

The dream goes with the setting of the sun, and the pine boles change from the red of hope and warmth to gray reality. Ethan and Mattie move toward their fateful ride. The sky is swollen with clouds, and Ethan's eyes are also clouded.

The flashback history of Ethan over, the narrative returns to the present, and the narrator begins to allay Mrs. Hale's fears that he had been buried in a snow drift in what was the worst blizzard of the winter. On this worst night of the year, the narrator has descended into his hell of cold and snow and has been resurrected with a new understanding of the meaning of the whiteness. Melville tells us in *Moby Dick* that there "lurks an elusive something in the innermost idea of this hue, which strikes more of panic to the soul than that redness which affrights in blood. . . . [Whiteness] heightens that terror to the furthest bounds." And again, "as in essence whiteness is not so much a color as the visible absence of color, and at the same time the concrete of all colors; it is for these reasons that there is such a dumb blankness, full of meaning, in a landscape of snows—a colorless, all-color of atheism from which we shrink."[1]

Like Melville's white world, Ethan and the narrator's is a world of numbing emotional deadness, of cold, of stark, all-consuming isolation, of granite outcroppings. It is hardly the Berkshire country described by Henry Ward Beecher as the "Lake District of America." Nor is it the spring thaws of Jewett, where even in a story entitled "The Town Poor," the atmosphere is quite different. The contrasts are striking.

Jewett's characters, two women who are out visiting, also come upon people whose fortunes are reversed. The two poor women are living on the charity of the town, in a garret room in an isolated farmhouse:

> The four cups were not quite full of cold tea, but there was a clean old tablecloth folded double, and a plate with three packs of crackers neatly piled, and a small—it must be owed, a very small—piece of hard white cheese. . . . Then there was a silence, and in the silence a wave of tender feeling rose high in the hearts of the four elderly women. At this moment the setting sun flooded the poor plain rooms with light; the unpainted wood was all of a

golden-brown, and Ann Bray, with her gray hair and aged face, stood at the head of the table in a kind of aureole.[2]

The story concludes with the two visitors vowing to make amends for the isolation of the two sisters and reaffirming the community's obligation to the poor. No such good fortune awaits Ethan; nor does he have the "refinement of character and self respect" so integral to Jewett's more benign New England. Melville's grim understanding of the absence of color haunts the story, and Jewett's warm, caring New England is not here.

Ethan Frome, then, is a story of cold, of snow, of a rock-hard existence. The setting becomes a metaphor for the limited possibilities of Ethan's physical and emotional life. It is a story of frozen passion locked in crippled bodies and devastated minds. But more than mere cold, the setting also captures the pervasive isolation of the citizens of Starkfield. As in most small towns, the inhabitants of Starkfield all know each other. The narrator also assures us that if we had spent even a brief time there we would also find the post office, and then Ethan. We would have asked who he was, and everyone would have known. Yet in Starkfield, acquaintance does not mean community. The inhabitants are not the idealized extended family. Mrs. Hale does go to visit the Fromes—and they were at one time good friends—but now she goes only twice a year. The narrator comes in to the village and quickly learns that he will always be only on the periphery of any real understanding of the inhabitants and that his understanding of the people and place will have to be drawn from scraps of information and his own inferences. He is a connection to the outside world—and his daily trips to the station emphasize this—but his journeys to and from are passed largely in silence. He rides with Ethan two hours a day for five days, but they exchange few words. (Certainly the story would have been a brief one had Ethan narrated it.) The narrator acts as our guide into the cold world, but what he sees does little to dispel our geographic chill.

The persuasive isolation of Ethan's environment is also marked in ways other than by the weather. Thomas Hardy in *Desperate Remedies* voices the belief that "there's a backward current in the world, and we must do our utmost to advance in order just to bide where we be." Ethan works as hard as he can, but the current is too strong. He notes that "we're kinder side-tracked here now." The railroad, a symbol in the development of America for connection, community, and communication, has just the opposite effect on Ethan's life. Before the railroad was built through to the Flats, people passed in front of Ethan's house. To the old Mrs. Frome's good fortune, when they were mending the railroad, Harmon Gow brought his stage by her place, and she had a reason for moving out of herself, at least to get down to the gate to see him. After the road was mended and the railroad built, Mrs. Frome had nothing to draw her out, and nobody came. She never could fully understand why the visits stopped, "and it preyed on her right along until she died." Ethan attributes the worst of his mother's troubles to the coming of the railroad, and his troubles parallel his mother's: his mother sickens, Zeena comes to nurse; his mother dies, Ethan marries Zeena. With brilliant irony, Wharton turns the coming of the railroad, historically the advent of mobility and expansion, into a catalyst for isolation and despair.

Ethan's situation is also a bitterly wry comment on other aspects of the American dream. Just as the railroad does not bring him wealth and escape, neither does Ethan inherit the upward mobility that is theoretically the American birthright. Instead of an ever-expanding farm, the deserved result of Ethan's endless labor, Ethan's house is losing to the current. The narrator first sees the house, and we are told that "the snow has ceased, and a flash of watery sunlight exposed the house on the slope above us in all its plaintive ugliness. The black wraith of a deciduous creeper flapped from the porch, and the thin wooden walls, under their worn coat of paint, seemed to shiver in the wind that had risen with the ceasing of the snow" (*EF*, 15). It is one of those "lonely New England farm houses that make the landscape lonelier" (*EF*, 15).

Ethan notes that the house was bigger in his father's time, but he has had to take down the L (we are never told why). Loss of the L is more than relinquishing closed space; the narrator tells us that an L often serves as the very heart of a house. Moreover, it protects the inhabitants from the harsh winter mornings, as they face their morning's work. Ethan's protection from the snow has been given up, and the cold of the climate has come inside.

The inside of Ethan's house offers little contrast to the barren outside. The kitchen is cold, requiring that inhabitants huddle near the stove. The furniture is rough wood, the furnishings sparse: "Three coarse china plates and a broken-nosed milk jug had been set on a greasy table scored with knife-cuts, and a couple of straw-bottomed chairs and a kitchen dresser of unpainted pine stood meagerly against the plaster walls" (*EF*, 128).

The food is equally unpalatable—the remains of a "cold mince pie in a battered pie dish." The women blend well with the surroundings. Zeena is wearing a slatternly calico wrapper and has a broken comb in her thin grey hair. Her skin is sallow; her eyes "reveal nothing and reflect nothing." Mattie is also bloodless and shriveled, amber skinned rather than sallow, her hair also grey. Her eyes, rather than blank, have a bright witchlike stare. Her body has a limp immobility. Even the hearth fire has gone out. The American dream has vanished.

Wharton's use of a setting here has often been called too heavy-handed, obvious, and unremittingly bleak. There is little question that if one reads the frame alone, the charges have some validity. But the cold squalor of Ethan's later life gains poignancy through the relief we are offered by the story itself; the pain of his existence is intensified by our knowledge of what has been. Before the L was lost, Ethan's environment was sparse but not desolate.

Wharton, then, skillfully uses the New England winter as a metaphor for Ethan's life, both past and present. We are never allowed to forget the chill of his life, and the snow creates the physical atmosphere for the mental anguish of the story. Other elements in the scenery are also used symbolically. Trees, for example, figure prominently, and not only as the ultimate instrument for destruction. We are told early on that the elm is dangerous and should be cut down. Ruth and Ned were nearly the victims: "Ned Hale and Ruth Varnum came just as *near* running into the big elm at the bottom. We were all sure they were killed" (*EF*, 35). The prediction of danger proves to be despairingly correct. But in addition to the most obvious use of the elm, references to other natural objects build a pattern of imagery that defines the freedom and passion of Mattie and Ethan when they are outside versus the stifling morality and deadness they suffer when they are inside the house. For example, two black Norway spruces provide the setting for the lovers' passion and their subsequent death pact. When they join each other, often after the church social, they stand "together in the gloom of the spruces, an empty world glimmering about them wide and grey under the stars" (*EF,* 34). Though unspoken, their mutual passion is intense, and the dark spruces provide the shelter for their feelings: "It was so dark under the spruces that he could barely see the shape of her head beside his shoulder. He longed to stoop his cheek and rub it against her scarf. He would have liked to stand there with her all night in the blackness" (*EF,* 34).

Later in the story, in Chapter 9, they again stand together, and though only three days have passed, their love has moved from inarticulated feelings to avowals of passion. Ethan guides Mattie toward the Norway spruces (*EF,* 120), and they realize that this is the place where Ned Hale and Ruth Varnum had kissed each other, a sight Ethan had happened upon just after Andrew Hale had turned down his request for the money that would have freed him to go with Mattie. Ethan's initial telling of the incident under the spruces, done on the one evening they spend alone together, does not move them into the intimacy Ethan had hoped for, but this time the mention of the kiss acts as a catalyst for Mattie's own feelings, and she kisses Ethan and pleads that they not separate. With the dark spruces silently watching, Ethan and Mattie agree to die together.

Even on the rare occasions when the trees bring cheerful recollections, Ethan sees them as a mockery of his situation. The night he ponders leaving Zeena, his emotions go from exhilaration to despair: first he hopes to leave, then he decides that he will never have the money. He moves to the couch, and tears come to his eyes. As he goes deep into himself and his sorrow, he looks out the window to see a "moon-suffused sky. A crooked-tree branch crossed it, a branch of the apple-tree under which, on summer evenings, he had sometimes found Mattie sitting when he came up from the mill." But rather than these memories giving relief, they only serve to sharpen the pain: "it seemed as though all the beauty of the night had been poured out to mock his wretchedness" (*EF,* 99).

Trees of summer are mocking; trees of lovers, equally derisive. Constantly, they are remembrances of things past, reminders of the prison he is in, or foreboding symbols of the destruction to come. The big elm threatens death and does maim. The dark spruces provide shelter for Mattie and Ethan who must hide their love, while providing cool shade for Ruth and Ned who can be open with theirs.

Trees, too, are Ethan's main source of livelihood—but it is a livelihood of back-breaking labor after the trees have been cut. The phallic implications of the felled trees are very clear, symbolizing the impotence Ethan feels when he is refused immediate payment for the trees, thus cutting off his only avenue of escape. Equally double-edged is the fact that Ethan connects Mattie's hair, "soft yet springy" as he presses his lips to it, with the "faint woody fragrance of fresh sawdust in the sun" (*EF,* 107–08). He longs to tell her that her hair "smelt of the woods" (*EF,* 114). Ethan is to feel the "soft and springy" hair once again at the bottom of the elm.

In conjunction with the tree imagery that is integral to the setting, Wharton also makes skilled use of butterflies, birds, even small animals, to define her characters and weave a complex structure into the story. For example, Wharton connects Mattie and Ethan's summer happiness with "surprising" a butterfly in the winter woods (*EF,* 113). When Ethan has to tell Mattie she must go, her lashes "beat his cheek like netted butterflies" (*EF,* 89).

The bird imagery in the story is even more pronounced. Mattie is associated in Ethan's mind with the lightness of birds in spring and with his possibilities for happiness. As Ethan and Mattie are talking about the dangers of the elms, Ethan notes that "the motions of her mind were as incalculable as the flit of a bird in the branches" (*EF,* 35), and he ponders his frustration; he has no right to express his feelings, and he can only guess at hers. Like a bird, she is as elusive as his happiness. When they are sharing their evening together, Ethan again associates Mattie and his happiness with her with birds: "her hands went up and down above the strips of stuff, just as he had seen a pair of birds make short perpendicular flights over the nest they were building" (*EF, 69*). Later, when Zeena has told Ethan that Mattie must leave, and Ethan is walking into Starkfield, all of his surroundings are alive with her presence. Realizing that his world depends on her, he determines to try to do something: "Once, in the stillness, the call of a bird in a mountain ash was so like her laughter that his heart tightened and then grew large; and all these things made him see that something must be done at once" (*EF, 103*).

What is done, of course, is much different than what Ethan anticipates here. Each of the bird references in the story is followed closely with a reference to Zeena and to Ethan's ties to her. When the thread of imagery runs to the fateful sleigh ride, Wharton skillfully binds her story together by references not to birds this time but to another helpless creature in the New England winter, field mice. The language Wharton uses to describe the sounds Ethan hears are reminiscent of the bird associations with Mattie—and, one could say, are more appropriate for birds than mice. After the crash, Ethan hears a "small frightened *cheep* like a field mouse" (italics Wharton's). Then he registers that "he felt rather than heard the twittering." Moments later he understands that the "twittering came from her lips" (*EF, 125*).[3]

References to trees, birds, and mice, therefore, are all image patterns connecting Mattie, and Ethan's love for her, with the natural freedom of the outdoors. In contrast, and a natural enemy to both birds and mice, is Zeena's domestic cat. Always inside, it is a sinister presence that continually appears as Zeena incarnate to remind Ethan of his duty and to act as a perverse counter to Ethan's happiness. The references to the cat are numerous and almost too obvious. The first mention of the cat occurs when Zeena has left to seek another medical opinion, and Ethan and Mattie are looking forward to an evening together. The kitchen scene is one of comfortable well-being, and the cat is dozing in the chair. When Ethan returns in early evening, the cat is still dozing by a bright fire. The symbolism intensifies as Mattie nearly trips over the cat as it rubs against her leg, and Ethan becomes suddenly jealous (*EF, 61*). Mattie reassures him that he is the source of her good mood, but the mention of Zeena quickly dispels that. The "cat, unbidden, jumped between them into Zeena's empty chair," and the connection is broken. The presence of the cat, next described as "greedy," quickly throws a pall over their brief happiness and becomes a catalyst for their tragedy: "The cat, unnoticed, had crept up on muffled paws from Zeena's seat to the table, and was stealthily elongating its body in the direction of the milkjug, which stood between Ethan and Mattie. The two leaned forward at the same moment and their hands met on the handle of the jug. Mattie's hand was underneath, and Ethan kept his clasped on it a moment longer than was necessary. The cat, profiting by this unusual demonstration, tried to effect an unnoticed retreat, and in doing so backed into the pickle-dish, which fell to the floor with a crash" (*EF*, 62).

After supper, the cat continues to plague them and embody Zeena. Mattie first sits in Zeena's chair, only to realize that she assumes Zeena's aura when she is in her place; she quickly moves. "The cat, who had been a puzzled observer of these unusual movements, jumped up into Zeena's chair, rolled itself into a ball, and lay watching them with narrowed eyes" (*EF*, 66).

The scene before the focus shifts to the cat is one of steadily building, though always unspoken, passion. Ethan and Mattie talk around their day, both independently aware of the warm tensions they share. They discuss briefly Zeena's attitude toward Mattie, then flee into avoidance, not thinking about it anymore. Ethan builds his courage and continually reaches for the "stuff" Mattie is working on, seeking a physical connection to her. She does not move her head as the emotional currents travel down the material, until the cat jumps to catch a mouse: "The cat had jumped from Zeena's chair to dart at a mouse in the wainscot, and as a result of the sudden movement the empty chair had set up a spectral rocking" (*EF*, 70). Ethan's mood is broken; he returns to the harsh reality of his life, and Mattie feels the shift. Rather than try to reestablish the connection, something both of them realize is hopeless, Ethan begins to put out the fire (both literally and figuratively), and Mattie drags the cat's bed toward the stove. Zeena has triumphed.

The next morning, Ethan feigns indifference to Mattie in front of Jotham Powell, and this time he throws scraps to the cat, who, instead of purring, is "growling at the weather" (*EF*, 73). But Ethan has symbolically made his choice. The next scene appears derisively calm. The table is carefully laid, the fire is burning, and the cat is dozing; but Zeena is home.

We next see the cat after Zeena has told Ethan that Mattie must leave. Ethan returns to the kitchen, and the cat, which had been curled up on Mattie's lap, leaps away and abandons Mattie, in favor of Zeena. The cat ingratiates itself now with Zeena, and Zeena throws it a scrap of meat from her plate (*EF,* 91), imitating the exact gesture Ethan had made when he had been pretending indifference to Mattie in front of Jotham.

The cat continues to be the structural connection throughout this crucial scene. Ethan and Mattie are in a desperate dance of desolation over their impending separation, the kitchen warmth only exacerbating their pain. Zeena leaves to look for medicine, and the cat returns to its fateful place in Zeena's rocking chair, assuring the couple of Zeena's presence even in her absence. Zeena returns to the room with the broken pickle-dish, and Ethan, with more truth than he knows, blames the destruction on the cat trying to catch a mouse that had been in the kitchen all last evening. Zeena credits the cat with intelligence but not enough to repair the broken dish. Mattie confesses, Zeena cruelly berates, Ethan retreats.

As the moment for Mattie's departure draws nearer and nearer, Zeena's behavior with her cat continues to reinforce the sense of her determination and, by association with Ethan's parallel gestures, his corresponding lack of it. Zeena gets up on the morning of Mattie's departure full of "unusual alertness and activity" (*EF,* 101). She feeds the cat, once again with leftover scraps, this time symbolically from the pie that Mattie had baked. When we last see Zeena before Ethan leaves to take Mattie to the station, she is in her rocking chair by the stove, a place she settles into after feeding the cat. When she reappears, almost 24 years later, the cat is gone; the battered pickle-dish remains.

The presence of the cat, then, is an important structural device for the story. While associated with warmth and well-being when on Mattie's lap, it is only a temporary resident there. It is Zeena's cat and is Zeena's essence. When Ethan throws it food, he does so deliberately to feign indifference to Mattie. Its sudden movement causes the dish to break and becomes the vehicle for catching Ethan in a lie. It chases a mouse and causes Zeena's chair to rock, recalling her presence and foreshadowing the crippled mouselike figure that wakes at the bottom of the elm.

Wharton has numerous other image patterns in the story, less dominant than the cat-mouse imagery. Flowers and plants, for example, though usually a symbol of bountifulness and nature's replenishment, in this novel of "granite outcroppings" only serve to emphasize the harshness of the land and of the lot of the people on it. When Ethan walks Mattie home, aglow with the warmth of her presence, his euphoria, his feeling of walking "as if they were floating on a summer stream" (*EF,* 38), is broken as he approaches the house and sees that a "dead cucumber-vine dangled from the porch like the crape streamer tied to the door for a death" (*EF,* 39). Ethan quietly wishes it were a wreath for Zeena and has a vision of her corpselike, her mouth open, her teeth out, as he walks by the "rigid gooseberry bushes" and tries to find a key into his own barren house.

Geraniums, too, figure prominently as reflections of the personalities of the two women in Ethan's life and are always noted in the presence of the cat, Zeena's surrogate. When aligned with Mattie, they underscore Ethan's happiness with her: "The sun slanted through the south window on the girl's moving figure, on the cat dozing in a chair, and on the geraniums brought in from the door-way, where Ethan had planted them in the summer to 'make a garden' for Mattie" (*EF,* 50).

Later, Mattie and Ethan are enjoying their evening together, while the cat is "watching them with narrowed eyes," the "faint sharp scent of the geraniums mingled with the odors of Ethan's smoke" (*EF,* 66). However, the "sharp scent" turns increasingly sour, as Mattie, now depressed that the evening is over, moves the cat's bed and lifts "two of the geranium pots in her arms, moving them away from the cold window. He followed her and brought the other geraniums, the hyacinth bulbs in a cracked custard bowl and the German ivy trained over an old croquet hoop" (*EF,* 71). What had been a pleasant summer garden now becomes the winter of their discontent.

After Zeena has returned from her trip, the setting is the same, but the scene is much different. With the cat in the rocking chair, the "heat of the fire was beginning to draw out the faint sharp scent of the geraniums" (*EF,* 92), recalling their former evening of joy. But now, Ethan and Mattie are clinging together desolately, and Ethan is dragging himself wearily to his feet, as Zeena returns with the broken pickle-dish.

When Mattie is packed and leaving, Zeena makes the final comment on the underlying symbolism of the flowers. Walking over to the window, she snips two or three yellow leaves and comments, "Aunt Martha's ain't got a faded leaf on 'em; but they pine away when they ain't cared for" (*EF,* 102). Ethan's careful planting and his and Mattie's moving them away from the window could not protect them from Zeena's withering touch.

Another integral part of the symbolic scenery of the novel is the object of the cat's destruction, the pickle-dish. Pickles, which come from cucumber vines, reminding us of Ethan's crape streamer, with their connotations of shriveled sourness are first mentioned by Zeena when she asks Mattie to save her empty medicine bottle and get the taste out of it for pickles (*EF,* 49). With more prescience than she knew, Aunt Philura Maple had given Ethan and Zeena a red glass pickle-dish for their wedding. Sadly, Zeena cherishes it in the only the way she knows how, by putting it on top of the china closet, out of reach, and out of harm's and life's way. Like the rest of her soured and stifled life, she only takes it down during spring cleaning, and then she "always lifted it with my own hands 'so's 't shouldn't get broke'" (*EF,* 93).

Mattie, conversely, has not lived her life on a shelf and, even while knowing she is touching forbidden fruit, takes the dish down to make a special table for Ethan. When the cat knocks the dish off, Mattie realizes immediately the importance of the breakage, while Ethan, significantly, does not even remember that the dish was a wedding gift. Ethan replaces the dish, broken but fragilely pieced together, and reassures Mattie that he has a plan for fixing it. He will get glue and repair it tomorrow, trust that Zeena will not notice it until next spring cleaning or at least for several months, and in the meantime will find a replacement in Shadd's Falls or Bettsbridge. Like all of his other dreams, this one too is fated to fail, and even more painfully so since he comes so close. He gets the glue but only after going to several stores, a delay that costs him the opportunity to repair it before Zeena returns. Zeena, looking for powders for her illness (again linking medicines with the pickles), finds the broken dish and, pathetically explaining its significance to her, links its fate with that of Mattie. Holding the shattered dish, she makes it a symbol for the wreckage of her life and what she intuitively knows is the loss of Ethan to Mattie: "'You're a bad girl, Mattie Silver, and I always known it. It's the way your father begun, and I was warned of it when I took you, and I tried to keep my things where you couldn't get at 'em—and now you've took—from me the one thing I cared for most of all.' She broke off in a short spasm of sobs that passed and left her more than ever like a shape of stone" (EF, 94). The "shape of stone," so like the granite outside, carries the broken glass out of the room "as if she carried a dead body."

The sexual significance of the pickle-dish also cannot be ignored. In his excellent analysis of the meaning of the dish, Kenneth Bernard argues that the dish is emblematic of Ethan's and Zeena's sexual life (Bernard, 178–84). The dish is Zeena's most prized wedding gift. She relegates it to ceremonial, not functional use. She has never yet found the occasion for ceremony. Mattie uses the pickle-dish, with its phallic contents, and it gets broken, never to be the same again. Zeena, understanding this intrusion for the irrevocable sacrilege that it is, cries out her own loss but never accepts the blame. For Zeena, the source of the sterility of her marriage will always lie in other people. She, in giving the empty medicine jar to Mattie to use for pickles, symbolically, albeit unwittingly, passes her sexuality on to Mattie—but Ethan's impotence makes the gesture a useless, broken one. The cucumber vine at the entrance to Zeena and Ethan's house is indeed a very dead one.

The red pickle-dish, then, when used by Mattie symbolizes life, vitality, warmth, security; in Zeena's hand it is repression, distance, covetousness, manifested in cold glass. This symbolic contrast of the two women is used by Wharton in several other image patterns throughout the novel. The red of the pickle-dish, which only comes to life with Mattie, is clearly Mattie's color. Ethan can easily discern which of the church dancers she is by the "cherry-colored" fascinator on her head (*EF*, 23). Or, when they arrive home that night to meet the resentful Zeena, Mattie has the "colour of the cherry scarf in her fresh lips and cheeks" (*EF*, 40). On the evening of her arrival, she had first appeared with a ribbon at her neck, eliciting a sarcastic stare from Zeena (*EF*, 58). Mattie also wears a streak of crimson ribbon the night of her dinner with Ethan; the ribbon "transformed and glorified her." At the only other time of real happiness for the couple, the summer picnic, Mattie has on a pink hat; and on her moving day, during the sleigh ride, Mattie has on her red scarf. At all the major events of their courtship—the meeting, the picnic, the dinner, the last ride—Mattie has on red; Zeena by contrast wears ugly yellow flannel (*EF*, 42). When the narrator sees the two women more than 20 years later, Zeena is still in a "slatternly calico wrapper." Mattie's red ribbons are gone; her hair is grey.

The gray hair that Mattie and Zeena share at the end of the novel is a blending of the color patterns that have appeared throughout the story. Always there is a contrast between the light, bright, hot, red world of Mattie, and the grey, dull, cold world of Zeena and Starkfield. The opening paragraph of the internal story sets this stage: "The village lay under two feet of snow, with drifts at the windy corners. In a sky of iron the points of the Dipper hung like icicles and Orion flashed his cold fires. The moon had set, but the night was so transparent that the white housefronts between the elms looked gray against the snow, clumps of bushes made black stains on it, and the basement windows of the church sent shafts of yellow light far across the endless undulations" (*EF*, 20). What could offer the clarity of black and white in Ethan's world always blends to grey. The black shade of the Varnum spruces becomes grey under the stars (*EF*, 34). The open country stretches "grey and lonely under the stars" as Ethan and Mattie wind their solitary way homeward (*EF*, 37). As Ethan looks out the window on Mattie's last day, he sees the grey fields (*EF*, 100).

It is this greyness that permeates all of Ethan's environment and reflects his inability to see clearly or act decisively. The opaqueness turns to clear black only when Ethan and Zeena first openly express their anger. As Ethan lights the candle in his bedroom, "Zeena's face stood grinning out against the uncurtained pane, which turned from grey to black." But the clarity is too late, the habits of inertia too strong, the implications of this anger too terrifying to face. The greyness wins; Zeena and Mattie are blended together when the narrator meets them, Zeena with "her thin grey hair . . . drawn away from a high forehead," and Mattie, "her hair as grey as her companion's, her face as bloodless and shriveled" (*EF*, 127).

The grey atmosphere of Starkfield is occasionally broken by red dawns and hearth fires, but rather than warmth and hope they offer only a disdainfully ironic comment on Ethan's life. The "cold fires of Orion" outline the dimensions of Ethan's dilemma, as his existence seems stifled by the oxymoron that is his life. Standing outside the church, Ethan can only observe the "volcanic fires" of the heaving dancers. Mattie's coming to his house is "like the lighting of a fire on a cold hearth." Ethan and Mattie return from the dance to a fire that has been out long ago; it becomes warm and inviting again only when Ethan and Mattie are alone before it. When the narrator is invited into Ethan's kitchen, the fire is out, and Mattie is whining about the cold.

Just as the hearth fire promises only illusionary warmth, so the sun gives little consolation. The sunset is "cold red" (*EF*, 26). The sun does rise bright in the sky, and Mattie's face becomes a part of the sun's red, but her reflection only intensifies the lonely helplessness Ethan feels. Finally, he awakes after his night of mourning for Mattie, and the chill of the winter dawn is in the room—the red sun is on the grey rim of the fields, rising on what is to be Mattie's last day (*EF*, 99–100).

Watching over all of Ethan's world is another recurring symbol that Wharton uses to comment on Ethan: Orion. Already noted is the reference to Orion's cold fires, and it is Orion that Ethan explains to Mattie as he subconsciously courts her on their walks together: "That's Orion down yonder; the big fellow to the right is Aldebaran, and the bunch of little ones—like bees swarming—they're the Pleiades" (*EF*, 26). Orion is an apt symbol for Ethan, with its connotations of failure and lost dreams. Ethan's guardian star, according to mythology, was originally a great hunter, a young man of huge stature and impressive beauty. He fell in love with the daughter of the king of Chios. The king promised him his daughter but kept delaying the match until Orion, frustrated and drunk, attacked the maiden. For his rashness he was blinded, but his sight was later restored by the rays of the sun. Another element of the myth has Orion pursuing the Pleiades, the daughters of Atlas, but always being thwarted. Zeus took pity on the women and made them stars. Orion, as a constellation, has persistently continued his unsuccessful chase.

Aldebaran, the second star Ethan mentions, is equally foreboding. While it is the brightest star in the constellation Taurus, it also follows the Pleiades in useless pursuit. To complete the ominous star pattern, Wharton also has Ethan look straight into the heavens immediately after the crash and vaguely try "to reckon whether it was Sirius," the brightest star in the sky and the dog star who celestially follows the ill-fated Orion.

Orion and his followers, then, form a symbolic cluster that overshadows Ethan's life. He describes them to demonstrate his learning to Mattie, with a poignant echo of his thwarted hopes for an education. Orion is his guardian as Ethan looks into the church that bright winter night (the time when the constellation is most prominent), once again an observer to the possibilities within; and Sirius stares at the maimed bodies at the front of the elm. In a deft touch Wharton ties the fate of the constellation to the fate of the lovers by naming Mattie's father Orion, whose failure and death bring Mattie to the Frome farm in the first place. Mattie and Ethan are indeed star crossed.

Mattie, Ethan, and Zenobia also have significant names. Mattie's name is the feminine of the Hebrew name Matthew, literally "gift of Jehovah"—exactly what Ethan sees her presence in his life to be. Zenobia, by contrast, derives from the Latin meaning, "pertaining to Jupiter" or Zeus. According to legend, she was the daughter of Zeus. She was also a third-century queen of Palmyra who conquered Egypt. Her ambition outran her prudence, and she was defeated and brought as a prisoner to Rome. Her name has now become a symbol of ruthless arrogance. Ethan's own name is bitingly ironic. Like Mattie's, it comes from the Hebrew and means "firmness and strength"—the two qualities that could have given Ethan his "gift from Jehovah."

Last names, too, are emblematic: Ethan's "Frome" reminds us of Ethan's need to escape, to be "from" Starkville but not "in" the bleak town. Zeena is aptly from the Pierce family, a name connoting sharpness and wounding. Mattie, of course, is Silver—twinkling, promising, sparkling. Again, the underlying irony enhances the tragedy.

Wharton uses all of these symbols to weave a tight structure for her story, holding together the disparate characters and strengthening the sense that they are inescapably entangled in a tragic web where every attempt at escape is only a fierce struggle that further entangles, further traps. Ethan wants to go to school, to escape the boredom of Starkfield; his mother's illness and death rein him in. Mattie offers him a glimpse of what could be, only to become what might have been. The narrator sees what is and will be until the principals are dead.

7

Philosophy

What, then, are we to derive from this grave tale of interminable suffering, where there is not "much difference between the Fromes up at the farm and the Fromes down in the graveyard; 'cept that down there they're all quiet, and the women have got to hold their tongues" (*EF*, 133). In this stark Greek tragedy, the Furies of *The Eumenides* do seem to forever pursue the lovers. But unlike Aeschylus's story, the suffering in Ethan is unredeeming. The Greek choral Furies, in contrast, are the pangs of conscience that lead us to remorse and ultimate self-fulfillment. They are that part of the human psyche that makes us fit inhabitants of the social order, that forces us into a sense of interconnectiveness. In the play they are fierce beings indeed:

> But black they are, and so repulsive.
> Their heavy, rasping breathing makes me cringe,
> And their eyes ooze a discharge, sickening,
> and what they wear—to flaunt *that* at the gods,
> the idols, sacrilege![1]

According to an ancient life of Aeschylus, at the first performance of the play, women miscarried and people fainted, so terrible was their visage and initial message. The Furies, however, do offer hope, and they do have a redeeming purpose. Because of them, Orestes seeks restoration, and Athena brings "Athens and human consciousness to birth." They are those motivating forces that, once met and conquered, bring us into a reverence for our own life (Aeschylus, 88, 90). As the play tells us:

> There is a time when terror helps,
> The watchman must stand guard upon the heart,
> It helps, at times, to suffer into truth. (Aeschylus, 254)

In *Ethan Frome,* however, the Furies are relentless, and the truth offers no recompense. Zeena is the Fury in Ethan's tragedy. Driven by her own frustrations and pain, she plagues Ethan both within and without. He cannot tolerate the thought of a lifetime of her presence, so he takes the fateful sled ride. But like her sisters before her, Zeena appears as his conscience just as he nears the tree. In this tragedy, however, the Furies do not give an exit song of "rejoice! rejoice—the joy resounds—all those who dwell in Athens, spirits and mortals, come." Nor do we "learn to praise your Furies, you will praise the fortunes of your lives" (Aeschylus, 275). In Wharton's novel, the Furies double; Mattie joins Zeena in the role, and the Greek exit song of joy, and any truth learned from suffering, becomes a "high thin voice," a whining complaint.

In *A Backward Glance,* Wharton notes that "life is the saddest thing there is, next to death; yet there are always new countries to see, new books to read (and I hope to write), a thousand little daily wonders to marvel at and rejoice in" (*BG,* 1063–64). The philosophy of *Ethan Frome* only includes the first half of this statement—and stops short of death. Lionel Trilling in "The Morality of Inertia" argues that Ethan's universe is cruelly incomprehensible:

> A certain propriety controls the literary representation of human suffering. This propriety dictates that the representation of pain may not be, as it were, gratuitous; it must not be an end in itself. The naked act of representing, or contemplating, human suffering is a self-indulgence, and it may be a cruelty. Between a tragedy

and a spectacle in the Roman circus there is at least this much similarity, that the pleasure both afford derives from observing the pain of others. A tragedy is always on the verge of cruelty. What saves it from the actuality of cruelty is that it has an intention beyond itself. This intention may be so simple a one as that of getting us to do something practical about the cause of the suffering or to help actual sufferers, or at least to feel that we should; or it may lead us to look beyond apparent causes to those which the author wishes us to think of as more real, such as Fate, or the will of the gods, or the will of God; or it may challenge our fortitude or intelligence or piety.

Trilling concludes that Mattie and Ethan "live in the moral universe of the Book of Job. In complex lives, morality does in some part determine destiny; in most lives it does not. Between the moral life of Ethan and Matty [*sic*] and their terrible fate we cannot make any reasonable connection. Only a moral judgement cruel to the point of insanity could speak of it as anything but accidental" (Trilling, 38, 43).

There is little doubt that Ethan's final predicament hardly fits his crime. Like Job, he must question the judgment of such unresolved and unrelieved suffering. Job's profound question of why he must suffer in this way is answered by a god who does not condescend to explain, who replies that God's judgment is not to be questioned. God appears to Job in the whirlwind to prove to him that there is meaning to life beyond what mere mortals can understand. Job then admits, "therefore have I uttered that I understood not; things too wonderful for me, which I knew not" (Job 42:3–6). Job repents in dust and ashes, and "the Lord gave Job twice as much as he had before," but in the stoney world of *Ethan Frome,* the doubling is of misery, not happiness.

Critics have said that Wharton lacked the vocabulary of happiness, and certainly *Ethan Frome* would support that contention. In the novel Wharton has explored with profound insight the moral dilemmas of the universe as she saw it. Throughout her career Wharton struggled with a major question: the seeming dichotomy between duty and individual happiness. The social system, including its customs, myths, religions, mores, and rituals, has evolved to give order to chaos. Social organizations are meant to exert controls over uninhibited, dangerous passions. Since there is, Wharton believed, no absolute eternal standard of manners, morals, truth, or beauty, human beings are defined by their social context and often crushed by the conflict between hopes and customs.

Wharton does not, however, preclude the role of free will for her characters. Ethan has the opportunity to choose to leave. Trapped by his own sense of guilt, and his inability to see beyond his immediate situation, he misses the opportunity for happiness. As it is for Robert Browning's Duke in "The Statue and the Bust," who fails to come on the appointed night to claim his love, the die is cast, the possibilities for fulfillment gone.

James Tuttleton, in his excellent essay "Edith Wharton, High Priestess of Reason" argues that in many respects Wharton's view of "the inexorability of cause and effect in human affairs is like that of George Eliot, whom she admired; one wrong deed, not righted, leads to another; one reaps what he sows; it is impossible to evade the consequences of an act, whether it is purposeful or accidental."[2]

Wharton recognizes, however, that heredity and environment also play a central role in one's moral choices. Consistently in her fiction Wharton shows the human will thwarted, ambitions destroyed, the human lot basically hopeless. Most of her characters are controlled by exterior social conventions. Ethan cannot bring himself to disavow his duty to his wife, no matter how much she may deserve it. However, for the most part Wharton would argue that such control, such devotion to duty, is necessary, for without it people would have no organized standard, no code, to live by. For Ethan to seek happiness would invite chaos. To remain with Zeena without Mattie is intolerable. The only clear option Ethan sees is death. But life is not fair, and Ethan does not die. He is left to live out his life in quiet desperation. Ethan becomes the embodiment of Wharton's belief that "given an indifferent universe, given a necessary social organization which may crush nonconformity, and given the incongruities which make of existence a tangled skein of ironies, the only acceptable philosophy of life is that of courageous resignation" (Tuttleton, 397).

Just how courageous Ethan is we can only surmise. We do know that he is resigned. From the first he is depicted as grave, taciturn. Harmon Gow tells us that he will most likely "touch a hundred," for the Fromes are tough. The narrator suggests what Ethan will look like at 100, "for he looks as if he was dead and in hell now" (*EF, 5*). Ethan chooses ethical conduct first and then tries to choose death. For his pains he is chained for life in a prison of incompatible people. With Mattie's presence constantly reminding him of what life could have been Ethan remains trapped in his marriage and tied to his farm. His ultimate horror is that he is not even allowed the bliss of ignorance. As Harmon says, the smart get away; Ethan is unable to even do that.

What, then, is the final taste of *Ethan Frome?* The pain of the story comes from its picture of lost hope, of lost potential. The terror of the story for any reader is its vision of people being imprisoned in lives of sterile expiation, with so little behind them and nothing before them. We have a lingering nightmare of days broken only by the night turning to day, of the sun also rising on lost lives. The black-white imagery that becomes the grey of the end of the story is made even more poignant by the life-giving spirit that Mattie in her red ribbons brings to Starkfield, only to lose. Pickles, the result of brine and aging, become the sour phallic symbol of the story; the broken dish the metaphor for shattered lives. Sickness prevails, and strength comes only through illness, and only to Zeena. The inertia that has been the story of Ethan's life is now the story of Mattie's too. The Fromes and the Silvers hang between Matthew Arnold's two worlds, one dead, the other powerless to be born; they can neither die nor really live.

What is left to the reader is indeed the route of the narrator—to get away. By looking at Ethan's life, we can reevaluate our own. Just as the Furies drive Orestes to a reevaluation and revitalization, so can Ethan's tableau force us to look our medusas in the face, take some comfort in having done so, and then take stock of the happiness remaining. Wharton did just that in writing out her despair at what can be the human lot. After looking at the horror, she moved on—but never quite left the "granite outcropping" she found in the "damp drizzly November of her soul." The real threat of *Ethan Frome* is that "troubles" can turn to "complications" at the swerve of a sled—that his life could become ours. We turn away from the novel, then, with a renewed sense that, given such possibilities, we must cherish even more the "thousand daily wonders" and rejoice in those "magical moments when the mere discovery that 'the woodspurge has a cup of three' brings not despair but delight" (*BG*, 1064).

Appendix

ETHAN FROME AS DRAMA

Ethan Frome, because of what it says about the human condition and because of its very spareness of style and economy of length, has remained one of Wharton's most popular stories. The bitter irony of her other novels is here, but the satiric lashes have given way to the clean brutal cuts of broken glass. Part of the novel's lasting popularity is also due to its dramatic potential. Recognizing this element, Owen Davis, a noted dramatic author, working in collaboration with his son, Donald, recast the novel as a play. It was presented in Philadelphia on 6 January 1936 and then published by Charles Scribner later in the same year with an introduction by Wharton herself.[1] Wharton praised the adaptation, though her own failing health prevented her from ever seeing the production. She says of the Davises' work, "Here at least is a new lease of life for 'Ethan' and the discovery moved me more than I can say." She continues: "I imagine few have had the luck to see the characters they had imagined in fiction transported to the stage without loss or alteration of any sort, without even the grimacing enlargement of gesture and language supposed to be necessary to 'carry' over the footlights" (Davis and Davis, viii).

Though Wharton was eminently satisfied with the results of the Davises' work, transforming the novel to the stage was a formidable job. Owen Davis, in his autobiographical *My First Fifty Years in the Theatre,* gives an intimate glimpse of the problems he faced.[2] He and his son had recently done a dramatization of Pearl Buck's *The Good Earth,* and both had an impressive list of screen plays and adaptations behind them. Owen Davis was on vacation when Jed Harris, a leading Broadway producer and director with an impressive list of stage credits, called and asked Davis about the theatrical potential of *Ethan.* Davis quickly reread the novel (he assured Harris that copies were readily available in all local New England libraries) and agreed to Harris's suggestion that he rewrite it as a play. He and Donald began to lay out the story line—but quickly realized that the narrative structure of the novel would pose particular problems for them:

> The story line was clear enough, and the characters were all drawn and were so real that they seemed actually to be alive, but as Miss Wharton wrote the story, it was all told to a stranger who had seen poor old Ethan, crippled and broken, dragging himself along the village street. It was the story of something that happened twenty years before and none of the characters, either of the book or of the play, told any of it. What they had done was clear enough but what they had said, it was up to us to write.
>
> Ethan Frome, his wife Zenobia, and little Mattie were glowing with life upon Mrs. Wharton's canvas, but she had given them no voices at all. It was a story of a very tender love, and of a hate so bitter that it could end only in a dreadful tragedy, but nowhere in the book was there a record of one single angry word. What Zenobia had said, and what Ethan had said, was sometimes briefly written down, but always in the words of some neighbor who was repeating it, but Mattie was only told about; what she had said and how she expressed herself Donald Davis and I had to work out ourselves. (Davis, 136–37)

Owen Davis soon had to go on to other projects, but Donald continued to work on the play for over a year, and though Jed Harris initially helped edit the play, his enthusiasm also waned, and he said he was unable to cast it. Davis then sought out Max Gordon, a major producer who had done his first independent Broadway production in 1930, and in two days Gordon had cast Raymond Massey as Ethan,

Appendix

Pauline Lord as Zeena, and Ruth Gordon as Mattie. Director Guthrie McClintic, who was married to Katharine Cornell, staged the play, and Joseph Mielziner did the scenery. Mielziner also had a formidable reputation in the theatre; after *Ethan Frome,* he did the sets for Katharine Cornell's *Saint Joan* and John Gielgud's *Hamlet.* (Sketches of his sets are included in the Scribner's edition of *Ethan Frome.*) The play opened in Philadelphia to fine reviews, but it was too expensive to make much money there. It then moved to New York for a triumphant four-month run at the National Theatre and had a longer career on the road. Richard Lockridge, the drama critic for the *New York Sun,* said of the play, "What was essential to Edith Wharton's *Ethan Frome,* the simplicity, the almost overpowering poignancy—is retained in the stage version, which was played at the National Theatre last evening, and the result is a tragedy which is deeply stirring and rather grimly beautiful. It is acted superlatively and gives the theatre, to say nothing of Max Gordon, a new cause for pride."[3]

Wharton was ultimately to do quite well financially from the dramatization of this play and of *The Old Maid,* which had won the Pulitzer Prize for drama in 1935. R. W. B. Lewis estimates that her earnings from these dramatizations from 1935 onward were more than $130,000—money she needed to support the large number of people dependent on her (Lewis, 529).

The dramatization of *Ethan,* then, was a commercial and artistic success, but to adapt it to the stage, the Davises had to make significant changes in the structure and, to a lesser degree, in the characterization. The play opens with a prologue—a dialogue between Harmon Gow and "a young man." Harmon takes the young man to Ethan's house, where the three of them haggle over the man's request to drive him to Corbury. Ethan agrees only after he learns he is to be paid, and Ethan is here depicted as being much more interested in money than he is in the novel—an emphasis that will continue throughout the play. In the play, for example, Ethan will sell his remaining cow to get money for Zeena's cure-all vibrator, and the couple's dialogues, recreated by the Davises, are often about their financial straits.

There are other subtle differences between the play and the novel, some of which can be ascribed to the fact that the filtering perspective of the narrator, a man who knows he is going to escape, is not omnipresent in the play. As a result, from the opening scenes the drama is even bleaker than Wharton's original harsh Starkfield winters.

The setting, for example, is relentlessly dreary. Though act 1, scene 1, opens in the spring, we are in the kitchen of the Frome house, which is already "a bleak and cold-looking place with an atmosphere of sordid poverty" (Davis and Davis, 15). There are unpainted cupboards, an old chair, "a geranium plant or two," and a "bleak early spring country landscape" (Davis and Davis, 16). Unable to enter Ethan's mind in the play, we are denied the protective patina of his imagination. Even the spring is bleak here.

The setting continues to underscore the helplessness of the characters' existence, long before the sled ride. Ethan and Zeena's bedroom is atticlike and bare. It has a cracked pitcher and bowl, a rickety bed, and a small table, "the top of which is littered with bottle, and pharmaceutical boxes and stained tumblers with spoons in them and various other patented medicine supplies" (Davis and Davis, 101–2). The cow is starving. The house, "flimsy with age," is sustained ugliness and penury. The scenes outside the window are always bleak springs and harsh winters. Jo Mielziner was praised for his staging. It is difficult to imagine a harsher environment than Wharton's novel, but the play manages it.

The symbolism that serves as such an important structural device in the novel is also present in the play but is necessarily much more subdued. The ambience is established by the stage sets, and the nuances of characters are the responsibility of the actors rather than narrative description. Nonetheless, the symbols that are transportable do appear. Geraniums are listed several times as the flower of choice for decorations: Mattie tends the flower, carrying it from the window to the stove as Ethan stands in helpless inarticulateness the night of their dinner together; later in the play Zeena accuses Mattie of neglecting it, prompting Mattie's anger at Zeena's unjust accusations. The cat, however, which figures so prominently in the novel, is replaced by a more manageable rocking chair, which Zeena always sits in, and it is this piece of furniture that serves as a reminder of her presence during Mattie's and Ethan's evening.

Appendix

Like the stage sets, characterization is also heightened in effect to meet the demands of the stage, but the integrity of the source is maintained. For example, Ethan is physically more impaired when we are introduced to him in the prologue. While he is visibly lame in the novel, in the play "his face is scarred, there is a huge deep gash across his forehead, and his right side is so warped that each step he takes costs him a visible effort" (Davis and Davis, 6). When he returns to his house, after agreeing to take the young man to his job, "he limps slowly and haltingly along the path, his forlorn figure silhouetted against the bleak snow landscape" (Davis and Davis, 12). The "careless powerful look" (*EF*, 3) is not here.

There are also subtle differences in his personality on stage from how he is imagined by the narrator in the novel. Because he must be more demonstrative to project "across the lights," there are more scenes of open emotion in the play. Consequently, the relationship with Zeena is overtly more tense. Ethan has to be argued into accepting Mattie into the house—Zeena uses her bad health and the fact that Mattie will cost very little extra as excuses. His emotional distance from Zeena is graphically illustrated when Mattie first shows him the pickle-dish, and here he says he has never even seen it before, though it was a wedding gift (Davis and Davis, 14). He openly voices his frustration with Zeena's presence: "she will be back here . . . this time tomorrow . . . rockin' away . . . creakin' and whinin' . . . (Davis and Davis, 169). He actually screams at Zeena when she says that she has lost her own health while nursing his mother and thus he should deny her nothing (Davis and Davis, 194). And the crucial scene in the novel where Ethan inquires questioningly if Zeena is going to send Mattie away is a violent explanation point in the play, but it is one that Ethan is unable to sustain (Davis and Davis, 201).

Finally, in the play, Ethan actually confronts Zeena with leaving. He tells her they are getting nowhere, that he would like to go west, that he will send her money as soon as he earns some. In the meantime, he will borrow money from Mr. Hale. It is the opening Zeena has waited for. She makes a brutal thrust:

ZEENA: Why, Ethan Frome–if you was in your right senses—you couldn't no more go an' take advantage of Andrew Hale bein' a good kind man—(*She stops rocking and looks at him closely*) Could you, Ethan? Hm? (*He glances at her and then away again— he couldn't and he knows it and he is being completely annihilated*) And if you did! Well—I guess't Mr. Hale ain't's big and fool's you think he is. D'you suppose he'd ever go and help you run off an' desert your poor sick wife who ain't hardly able to stand up— a woman who's worked and slaved for you, an' your mother before you? Andrew Hale, a man who's a deacon in the church and I don't know what all!—Now would he do a thing like that? Would he, Ethan? (*She rises—sets the empty cup in the sink—conscious that she is in complete control of herself and* ETHAN) If you got any sense at all—you'll buckle down and tend to your business and stop all this stuff'n nonsense! (Davis and Davis, 226)

And all of this takes place in the play *before* the broken pickle-dish is discovered.

As Ethan's anger and frustration with Zeena are more pronounced, so is his attraction to Mattie more obvious. He, for example, voices his jealousy of Denis Eady. When Denis asks if Ethan would mind him taking Mattie home, Ethan replies, "Yes—I will—but it's up to her" (Davis and Davis, 65). He also directly assures Mattie, as early as act 1, scene 3, that he would marry her if he could (Davis and Davis, 86). Later, in act 2, scene 2, (137) the tension of attraction between them is expressed in their natural awkwardness during a discussion about Zeena. Subsequently, he brings Mattie a gift when he goes shopping. Most important, it is long after they have recognized their love for each other, and while Ethan is touching her during the supper scene, that the pickle-dish is broken. The stage direction notes:

(They reach out simultaneously for the stack of dishes . . . and his hand falls on top of hers . . . he lets it stay there for a moment . . . then she is suddenly terribly self-conscious. . . . she pulls her hand from under his quickly . . . and her elbow knocks the red glass pickledish to the floor . . . it crashes and breaks . . . Mattie stares down at it . . . and murmurs) (Davis and Davis, 163).

What is accomplished by the cat in the novel is done by Mattie's own elbow in the play, as a direct result of their unspoken feelings for each other. While Ethan is more expressive of both his love and his hate in the play, he is not the stronger for it. Rather, the venting of his rage only emphasizes his impotence before it. He confronts Zeena and still withdraws; he knows he and Mattie love each other as early as act 1, yet he can do nothing. However, in the play he does have an even more formidable foe in Zeena than he has in Wharton's novel.

Dramatically, Zeena is not only a silent witch who uses her reticence and illness as a weapon; she also lashes out viciously when she does speak. All of Mattie's early attempts at friendship are rebuffed; instead, Zeena enjoys bossing her. She encourages Mattie to marry Denis, knowing she does not love him, warning that "paupers can't be choosey, Mattie" (Davis and Davis, 117). Mattie attempts to help Zeena pick up her clothes, and Zeena vehemently warns her never to "touch none of my things," a foreshadowing of the pickle-dish incident. She chastises Mattie for gazing fondly at Ethan. When Ethan pleads with Zeena that she not take the last penny they have left in the world, earned by selling the cow, she retorts: "Nonsense! Why, of course I can, Ethan . . . you ain't that mean!" (Davis and Davis, 132), and she uses the money for another doctor. She accuses Ethan of breaking her health; she is callously casual about sending Mattie away; she imperiously orders Mattie around. She twists every kind action of Ethan's and Mattie's into a perceived affront. She taunts Ethan's manhood and ridicules his attempts to provide for her:

> ZEENA: A-yeah! I been noticin' how you been neglectin' the farm lately . . . hangin around here helpin' Mattie sweepin' and scrubbin' floors . . . gettin' to be a regular old woman . . . ain't you, Ethan? Hm? (*She sups again and says firmly*) And you been cryin' over every mouthful we've 'et and complainin' how poor you are . . . Well . . . I only hope't you'll get a little work done once the new girl gets settled. (Davis and Davis, 222–23)

When Ethan finally defies her, she feigns a major attack:

> ZEENA: First that pie of yours like to knock me down, Matt, and now . . . Ethan settin' himself against me . . . and gettin' me all riled inside . . . (*She leans back against the cupboard and gasps*) I can't breathe! I can't breathe!
>
> MATTIE: (*Frightened*) Should I get you somethin', Zeena?
>
> ZEENA: I'll be all right . . . (*She holds one hand tight against her heaving chest . . . and with the other hand, drags a chair over to the cupboard . . . acutely conscious that* ETHAN *and* MATTIE *are watching her every move*) I should've tried that stomach powder last night when I said I would . . . I shouldn't never've tried to stand out against a heartburn like I got! (Davis and Davis, 232–33)

The only time she cries in her life, after finding the broken pickle-dish, is followed immediately by "intense and bitter hatred." She lashes at Mattie: "You're a no-good girl, Mattie Silver, and I've always known so." With her wonderful talent for distortion, she continues: "I was warned against you when I took you in here out of the kindness of my heart" (Davis and Davis, 236). The kindness of Zeena's heart has long ago turned bitter as bile. She is over silent in the novel; when she speaks in the play, we are appalled by the hearing.

Since the dramatic anger of the play is largely between Zeena and Ethan and, to a lesser degree, between Zeena and Mattie, Mattie's character does not receive the same embellishment of emotion that Zeena's and Ethan's do. Though admirably played by Ruth Gordon (Lockridge says of her part, "there is a kind of poetry in the character of Mattie"), she is the least complex of the major characters. The most open and forthright person in the novel, she continues to be so in the play. She is consciously solicitous of Zeena in both mediums, though she understands Zeena's malignity and tries to help Ethan understand it. She knows of her feelings for Ethan long before he acknowledges them and thus is ready to respond when Ethan becomes aware. She also serves as a touchstone for morality in the story; as one treats

Mattie, so does one treat the world. She is good in an evil world, both in the play and in the novel. When faced with banishment and desolation, she suggests suicide as the only way she can see to control her destiny. The only crucial metamorphosis for Mattie comes in the epilogue—and it is an added twist indeed.

In the novel, our final view of Mattie is of an old woman who is complaining about the dying fire, blaming Zeena for her chill: "It's on'y just been made up this very minute. Zeena fell asleep and slep' ever so long, and I thought I's be frozen stiff before I could wake her up and get her to 'tend to it" (*EF*, 128). In the play, she has made the transformation into Zeena with grotesque finality. She accuses Zeena of hurting her when Zeena moves her wheelchair into the room and tells Zeena: "I wish you'd let me die. Why didn't you let me die that night they carried Ethan an' me in here!" (Davis and Davis, 259). Then, when Ethan tries to help her, she brutally turns on him and leaves us with the final bitter taste:

MATTIE: No! Don't you touch me! Zeenie—you do it. He's so clumsy—he always hurts me! (ZEENA *takes the blanket from* ETHAN *who sinks back into the chair,* ZEENA *tucks the blanket about* MATTIE)

ZEENA: Shush—Shush—You're worse'n a baby, Mattie!

MATTIE: (*Flares up—querulously*) I can't stand havin' him touch me! (*She lurches her head about toward* ETHAN) Ain't you never goin' to die Ethan Frome?

ETHAN: (*Sits motionless—facing her*) The Fromes're tough, I guess. The doctor was sayin' to me only the other day—"Frome," he says, "you'll likely touch a hundred!" (Davis and Davis, 210).

Setting, symbolism, and characterization, then, are true to Wharton's basic conception of her story, though each area is intensified to embrace the dramatic tension of the play. The major themes of the story are also skillfully incorporated. The reticence of Ethan is emphasized by the repetitious "A-yeah" that he answers to many queries. Ethan tells Mattie of his mother's silence and his consequent marriage. The sounds of Zeena's silence are also here. Mattie tells Ethan of Zeena: "If she'd only tell me what I don't do right . . . but she don't hardly say a word for days" (Davis and Davis, 84). Mattie is repeatedly frightened by Zeena's silence and rigidity. Ethan tells us "how she don't say so much as a word—for days and days—and all the time them little things that don't amount to a hill of beans, keeps poisonin' her till sooner or later she's just got to bust loose!" (Davis and Davis, 126). And Zeena's silence infuriates Ethan much more in the play than we know of in the novel, perpetrating the outbursts of anger that Ethan is allowed in the stage production:

> ETHAN: (*Determinedly—after a pause*) I guess we've talked about this more'n enough . . . so's you know . . . no matter what you say . . . I can't afford a hired girl. (*She is eating absorbedly and doesn't reply . . . her silence infuriates him*) I said . . . I ain't got the money to pay a hired girl! (Davis and Davis, 197)

Zeena's illness is also central to the play and takes on an even more sinister aspect as she uses it to force Ethan to sell the cow, litters the house with bottles, and constantly complains of her condition. The omnipresence of her sickness is revealed in a scene not in the novel:

> MATTIE: I had an awful funny dream last night. You know what I dreamed? I dreamed Zeena come downstairs sayin' she was feelin' better and for a while this mornin' I didn't know if it was a dream or not . . . till I heard her!
>
> ETHAN: Feelin' better! (*There is a pause—then he adds*) Well, that's one thing I ain't never heard her complain about! (Davis and Davis, 73–74).

Ethan bitterly summarizes when he says to Mattie: "Zeena always was a great hand for sickness, and doctorin" (Davis and Davis, 91–92). Lockridge says of the dramatic Zeena, "Pauline Lord plays the wife, and her special method has never proved more effective than as she creates that soft, implacable woman, who crushed everyone with her weakness" (Lockridge, 26).

The helpless hopelessness of the novel also permeates the drama. The final sledding scene is more focused on the stage and is more simplistic. Since we are denied entry into Ethan's mind, the face of Zeena that causes him to swerve in the book is absent on the stage. Moreover, here Ethan and Mattie go down the hill side by side, "head first and together . . . holdin' each other tight. I want to feel you holdin' me!" The sledding scene reads:

MATTIE: (*A murmur*) Is it goin' to hurt, Ethan?

ETHAN: Don't be a scared, Matt . . . it ain't goin' to hurt . . . it ain't goin' to hurt at all . . . we're goin' to fetch that elm so hard we won't feel anything at all . . . exceptin' only each other! (*He stretches out at her side and their arms go around each other. . . . As he lurches the sled forward and it hangs momentarily upon the crest of the sheer drop . . . he murmurs*) Matt . . . Matt . . .

MATTIE: Hold me . . . hold me tight, Ethan! (*The sled plunges down over the drop and is gone . . .*) THE LIGHTS DIM OUT (*The sled is heard in the darkness . . . bounding faster and faster. . . .*) (Davis and Davis, 250–51).

The epilogue is brief—approximately 30 lines long—and the young man does not reenter. Mrs. Hale's commentary on the story is absent, the narrator's escape is not open to us, and the principal characters are left wishing for a death that will not come soon. The audience must have left the theater severely depressed, thankful to walk out into the night and away from the nightmare—but also deeply moved by the infinite possibilities for tragedy available to us all. If so, Wharton's hopes for the play were accomplished: "[that] my poor little group of hungry lonely New England villagers will live again for awhile on their stony hillside before finally joining their forebears under the village headstones. . . . I have lived among them, in fact and in imagination, for more than ten years, and their strained starved faces are still near to me" (Davis and Davis, viii).

Notes and References

1. Historical Context

1. I am indebted to R. W. B. Lewis's excellent biography for the details of Wharton's life. See R. W. B. Lewis, *Edith Wharton: A Biography* (New York: Harper & Row, 1975); hereafter cited in text.

2. *Edith Wharton: Novellas and Other Writings: Madame de Treymes, Ethan Frome, Summer, Old New York, The Mother's Recompense, A Backward Glance* (New York: The Library of America, 1990), 1124–26. All page references in the text to *A Backward Glance* are to this edition; hereafter cited in text as *BG*.

3. Critical Reception

1. R. W. B. Lewis and Nancy Lewis, eds., *The Letters of Edith Wharton* (New York: Macmillan, 1988), 256. All references to her letters are from this edition; hereafter cited in text as *Letters*.

2. F. T. Cooper, "Ethan Frome," *Bookman* 34 (November 1911): 312.

3. "Review of Ethan Frome," *Nation* 93 (26 October 1911): 396–97.

4. "Three Lives in Supreme Torture," *New York Times Book Review* (8 October 1911): 603.

5. "Half A Dozen Stories," *Outlook* 99 (21 October 1911): 405.

6. Henry Seidel Canby, "Edith Wharton," *Saturday Review of Literature* 14 (21 August 1937): 6–7.

7. Percy Lubbock, "The Novels of Edith Wharton," *Quarterly Review* 223 (1915): 195.

8. William Lyon Phelps, *The Advance of the English Novel* (New York: Dodd Mead & Co., 1915), 295; hereafter cited in text.

9. This Modern Library introduction is reprinted in *Novellas and Other Writings*, 114–26; hereafter cited as "Intro."

10. Abigail Ann Hamblen, "Edith Wharton in New England," *New England Quarterly* 38 (1965): 240; hereafter cited in text.

11. Bernard De Voto, "Introduction to *Ethan Frome*" (New York: Charles Scribner's Sons, 1938); reprinted in Blake Nevius, ed., *Edith Wharton's "Ethan Frome": The Story with Sources and Commentary* (New York: Charles Scribner's Sons, 1968), 91–93; page references are to this edition.

12. Lionel Trilling, "The Morality of Inertia," in his *A Gathering of Fugitives* (New York: Harcourt Brace Jovanovich, 1956), 34–44; hereafter cited in text.

13. Irving Howe, "Introduction: The Achievement of Edith Wharton," in *Edith Wharton: A Collection of Critical Essays* (Englewood Cliffs, N.J.: Prentice Hall, 1962), 5.

14. E. K. Brown, "Edith Wharton" and "Edith Wharton the Art of the Novel," reprinted in Howe's *Edith Wharton: A Collection of Critical Essays* (Englewood, N.J.: Prentice Hall, 1962), 62–72, 95–102; hereafter cited in text.

15. Blake Nevius, *Edith Wharton: A Study of Her Fiction* (Berkeley: University of California Press, 1953), 110, 118. The entire chapter, pp. 99–126, offers excellent insights on Wharton's fiction.

16. John Crowe Ransom, "Characters and Character: A Note on Fiction," *American Review* 6 (January 1936): 271–88; reprinted in Nevius, *Edith Wharton's "Ethan Frome,"* 89; references are to this edition.

17. Alfred Kazin, "Afterward," in *Ethan Frome* (New York: Macmillan, 1987), 131–39; *On Native Grounds* (Garden City, N.Y.: Doubleday & Co., 1942), 60; hereafter cited in text.

18. Gary Lindberg, *Edith Wharton and the Novel of Manners* (Charlottesville: University Press of Virginia, 1975), 50; Margaret McDowell, *Edith Wharton* (Boston: Twayne, 1976); Richard Lawson, *Edith Wharton* (New York: Frederick Ungar, 1977).

19. Cynthia Griffin Wolff, *A Feast of Words: The Triumph of Edith Wharton* (New York: Oxford University Press, 1977); Elizabeth Ammons, *Edith Wharton's Argument with America* (Athens: University of Georgia Press, 1980); hereafter cited in text.

20. Carol Wershoven, *The Female Intruder in the Novels of Edith Wharton* (Rutherford, N.J.: Fairleigh Dickinson University Press, 1982).

21. David Holbrook, *Edith Wharton and the Unsatisfactory Man* (New York: St. Martins Press, 1991), 20, 96.

4. Style

1. Millicent Bell, *Edith Wharton and Henry James: The Story of Their Friendship* (New York: George Braziller, 1965), 264–65, 290.

2. Edith Wharton, "The Writing of Ethan Frome," in *The Colophon: The Book Collection Quarterly* 1 (1932); reprinted in Nevius, *Edith Wharton's "Ethan Frome,"* 72–73.

3. W. D. MacCallan, "The French Draft of Ethan Frome," *Yale University Library Gazette* 27 (1952): 38–47.

4. Edgar Saltus, ed., *After-Dinner Stories from Balzac* (New York: Brentano's, 1888), 127–61; quotation is on p. 138.

5. Edith Wharton, *Ethan Frome* (New York: New American Library, Signet Classic Edition, 1986), 130. Introduction by Cynthia Griffin Wolff. All references to *Ethan Frome* are from this edition; hereafter cited in text as *EF*.

5. Characterization

1. Cynthia Griffin Wolff, "Cold Ethan and 'Hot Ethan,'" *College Literature* 14 (1987): 231; hereafter cited in text. I am indebted to Wolff's cogent discussion of the biographical elements in *Ethan Frome*.

2. Edwin Bjorkman, *Voices of Tomorrow: Critical Studies of the New Spirit in Literature* (New York: Mitchell Kennerley, 1913), 297.

3. Steven Penrod, ed., *Social Psychology* (Englewood Cliffs, N.J.: Prentice Hall, 1986), 174–178; hereafter cited in text.

4. Ernest J. McCormick, *Human Factors Engineering* (New York: McGraw-Hill, 1964), 565.

5. David Eggenschwiler, "The Ordered Disorder of *Ethan Frome*," *Studies in the Novel* 9 (1977): 237–46.

6. Kenneth Bernard, "Imagery and Symbolism in *Ethan Frome*," *College English* 23 (1967): 178–84; hereafter cited in text.

7. Jean F. Blackall, "The Sledding Accident in *Ethan Frome*," *Studies in Short Fiction* 21 (1984): 145–46.

8. Theodore Dreiser, *Sister Carrie* (Columbus, Ohio: Charles E. Merrill Publishing Co., 1969), 83.

9. John S. Haller and Robin M. Haller, *The Physician and Sexuality in Victorian America* (Urbana: University of Illinois Press, 1974), 297; hereafter cited in text.

10. Sarah Stage, *Female Complaints: Lydia Pinkham and the Business of Women's Medicine* (New York: W. W. Norton, 1979), 146.

11. F. E. Oliver, "The Use and Abuse of Opium," *Report of the State Board of Health of Boston*, 3 (1872): 768; excerpts reprinted in Haller and Haller.

12. Edith Wharton, *The House of Mirth, The Reef, The Custom of the Country, The Age of Innocence* (New York: The Library of America, 1983), 303.

13. Carroll Smith-Rosenberg, "The Hysterical Woman: Sex Roles and Role Conflict in 19th Century America," *Social Research* 39 (1972): 661–62.

14. Edward Sagarin, *Raskolnikov and Others: Literary Images of Crime, Punishment, Redemption and Atonement* (New York: St. Martin's Press, 1981), 101.

15. Geoffrey Walton, *Edith Wharton: A Critical Interpretation,* 2d ed., rev. (Rutherford, N.J.: Fairleigh Dickinson University Press, 1982), 86.

16. Ruth Rosen, *The Lost Sisterhood: Prostitution in America, 1900–1918* (Baltimore: The Johns Hopkins University Press, 1983), 147–57.

6. Setting and Symbolism

1. Herman Melville, *Moby-Dick: Or, The Whale,* ed. by Charles Feidelson, Jr. (New York: The Bobbs-Merrill Co., 1964), 255, 264.

2. Willa Cather, ed., *The Best Short Stories of Sarah Orne Jewett* (Boston: Houghton Miffin Co., 1924), vol. 2, 242–44.

3. For a summary of this imagery see Joseph X. Brennan, "Ethan Frome: Structure and Metaphor," *Modern Fiction Studies* 7 (1961–62): 347–56.

7. Philosophy

1. Aeschylus, *The Oresteia* (New York: Penguin Books, 1977), 233; hereafter cited in text.

2. James Tuttleton, "Edith Wharton, High Priestess of Reason," *Personalist* 47 (1966): 394; hereafter cited in text.

Appendix

1. Owen Davis and Donald Davis, *Ethan Frome: A Dramatization of Edith Wharton's Novel* (New York: Charles Scribner's Sons, 1936); hereafter cited in text.

2. Owen Davis, *My First Fifty Years in the Theatre* (Boston: Walter H. Baker Co., 1950), 135–139; hereafter cited in text.

3. Richard Lockridge, review of *Ethan Frome,* dramatized by Owen Davis and Donald Davis, *New York Sun,* 22 January 1936, p. 26; hereafter cited in text.

Bibliography

Chronological List of Works by Edith Wharton

Novels and Collections of Short Stories

The Greater Inclination. 1899
The Touchstone. 1900
Crucial Instances. 1901
The Valley of Decision. 1902
Sanctuary. 1903
The Descent of Man and Other Stories. 1904
The House of Mirth. 1905
The Fruit of the Tree. 1907
Madame de Treymes. 1907
The Hermit and the Wild Woman and Other Stories. 1908
Tales of Men and Ghosts. 1910
Ethan Frome. 1911
The Reef. 1912
The Custom of the Country. 1913
Xingu and Other Stories. 1916
Summer. 1917
The Marne. 1918
The Age of Innocence. 1920
The Glimpses of the Moon. 1922

A Son at the Front. 1923
Old New York. 1924
The Mother's Recompense. 1925
Here and Beyond. 1926
Twilight Sleep. 1927
The Children. 1928
Hudson River Bracketed. 1929
Certain People. 1930
The Gods Arrive. 1932
Human Nature. 1933
The World Over. 1936
Ghosts. 1937
The Buccaneers. 1938

Poetry

Verses. 1878
Artemis to Actaeon and Other Verse. 1909
Twelve Poems. 1926

Nonfiction

The Decoration of Houses. 1897
Italian Villas and Their Gardens. 1904
Italian Backgrounds. 1905
A Motor Flight through France. 1908
Fighting France, from Dunkerque to Belfort. 1915
French Ways and Their Meaning. 1919
In Morocco. 1920
The Writing of Fiction. 1925
A Backward Glance. 1934

Translations

The Joy of Living by Hermann Sudermann. 1902

Compilations

The Book of the Homeless. 1916
Eternal Passion in English Poetry. 1939

Bibliography

Letters

The Letters of Edith Wharton, ed. R. W. B. Lewis and Nancy Lewis. 1988.

Primary Sources

Lewis, R. W. B., and Nancy Lewis, eds. *The Letters of Edith Wharton.* New York: Macmillan Publishing Co., 1988.

Wharton, Edith. *Ethan Frome.* New York: New American Library, Signet Classics Edition, 1986. Introduction by Cynthia Griffin Wolff. Page references are to this volume.

—. *The House of Mirth, The Reef, The Custom of the Country, The Age of Innocence.* New York: The Library of America, 1985.

—. *Madame de Treymes, Ethan Frome, Summer, Old New York, The Mother's Recompense, A Backward Glance.* New York: The Library of America, 1990.

Secondary Sources

Books

Ammons, Elizabeth. *Edith Wharton's Argument with America.* Athens: University of Georgia Press, 1980. Argues that *Ethan Frome* is a study of fairy tale fantasy, bringing together the witch, the silvery maiden, and the woodcutter in a psychosexual drama in which the witch wins.

Auchincloss, Louis. *Edith Wharton.* Minneapolis: University of Minnesota Press, 1961. Short introductory treatment of life and major novels.

Bell, Millicent. *Edith Wharton and Henry James: The Story of Their Friendship.* New York: George Braziller, 1965. Biography of their friendship and literary relationship, which existed from approximately 1903 to 1916.

Bjorkman, Edwin. *Voices of Tomorrow: Critical Studies of the New Spirit in Literature.* New York: Mitchell Kennerley, 1913. Sees *Ethan Frome* as social commentary because it is too painful to view characters as individual sufferers.

ETHAN FROME

Davis, Owen. *My First Fifty Years in the Theatre*. Boston: Walter H. Baker Co., 1950. Provides background material for the dramatization of *Ethan Frome*.

Davis, Owen, and Donald Davis. *Ethan Frome: A Dramatization of Edith Wharton's Novel*. New York: Charles Scribner's Sons, 1936.

Goodman, Susan. *Edith Wharton's Women: Friends and Rivals*. Hanover, N.H.: University Press of New England, 1990. Analysis of the female characters' connections with other women, highlighting the pertinent interactions with Wharton's life. In *Ethan Frome*, Edith's mother is Zeena, Wharton and her father are Mattie and Ethan.

Haller, John S., and Robin M. Haller. *The Physician and Sexuality in Victorian America*. Urbana: University of Illinois Press, 1974. Helpful for its study of patent medicines of the period.

Hapke, Laura. *Girls Who Went Wrong: Prostitutes in American Fiction, 1885–1917*. Bowling Green, Ohio: Bowling Green State University Popular Press, 1989. Helpful historical material.

Holbrook, David. *Edith Wharton and the Unsatisfactory Man*. New York: St. Martin's Press, 1991. A Freudian approach to Wharton's supposedly incestuous relationship with her father.

Howe, Irving, ed. *Edith Wharton: A Collection of Critical Essays*. Englewood Cliffs, N. J.: Prentice Hall, 1962. Includes Blake Nevius's essay "On *Ethan Frome*," Lionel Trilling's "The Morality of Inertia," E. K. Brown's "Edith Wharton," and Edith Wharton's "The Art of the Novel."

Kazin, Alfred. *On Native Grounds*. Garden City, N.Y.: Doubleday & Co., 1942.

Lawson, Richard H. *Edith Wharton*. New York: Frederick Ungar, 1977. Introductory text providing a biographical summary and critical commentary on major novels and short stories. Concludes that Wharton's special gifts are in setting and style.

Lewis, R. W. B. *Edith Wharton: A Biography*. New York: Harper & Row, 1975. The definitive biography to date of her work, drawing on his access to the Wharton papers at Yale, opened in 1969.

Lindberg, Gary H. *Edith Wharton and the Novel of Manners*. Charlottesville: University Press of Virginia, 1975. Wharton's novels of manners, including *Ethan Frome*, are accounts of characters operating within an unexpectedly troubling network of habits and patterns that constitute their culture.

Lubbock, Percy. *Portrait of Edith Wharton*. New York: Appleton-Century Croft, 1947. An informal, biased memoir.

Lyde, Marilyn. *Edith Wharton: Convention and Morality in the Work of a Novelist*. Norman: Oklahoma University Press, 1959. Study of

Bibliography

Wharton's conception of the relationship between social conventions and morality. In *Ethan Frome* Zeena is the burden society has imposed on Ethan by trapping him into a loveless marriage.

McCormick, Ernest J. *Human Factors Engineering.* New York: McGraw-Hill, 1964. Helpful for its discussion of isolation.

McDowell, Margaret. *Edith Wharton.* Boston: Twayne, 1976. A comprehensive introductory survey, arguing that Wharton continued to explore new techniques, genres, and subject matter until just before her death. Six pages are devoted to *Ethan Frome,* affording a concise survey of major themes.

Nevius, Blake. *Edith Wharton: A Study of Her Fiction.* Berkeley: University of California Press, 1953. An early study of Wharton's fiction. Sees *Ethan Frome* as a study of "the trapped sensibility."

—. *Edith Wharton's "Ethan Frome": The Story with Sources and Commentary.* Edited by Blake Nevius. Scribner Research Anthologies. New York: Charles Scribner's Sons, 1968. An early collection of articles and resource material designed as a student guide to the novel.

Penrod, Steven, ed. *Social Psychology.* Englewood Cliffs, N. J.: Prentice Hall, 1986. Helpful for its discussion of the effects of loneliness.

Phelps, William Lyon. *The Advance of the English Novel.* New York: Dodd Mead & Co., 1915. A pejorative view of Wharton's work, though he grants that *Ethan Frome* is the best of a bad lot. He was later to change his opinion of Wharton.

Rosen, Ruth. *The Lost Sisterhood: Prostitution in America, 1900–1918.* Baltimore: The Johns Hopkins University Press, 1983. Helpful for historical material on Mattie's possible fate.

Sagarin, Edward. *Raskolnikov and Others: Literary Images of Crime, Punishment, Redemption and Atonement.* New York: St. Martin's Press, 1981. Good for its analysis of Zeena's and Ethan's responses to their fate.

Stage, Sarah. *Female Complaints: Lydia Pinkham and the Business of Women's Medicine.* New York: W. W. Norton, 1979.

Trilling, Lionel. *A Gathering of Fugitives.* New York: Harcourt Brace Jovanovich, 1956. Contains his excellent essay "The Morality of Inertia."

Vita-Finzi, Penelope. *Edith Wharton and the Art of Fiction.* New York: St. Martin's Press, 1990. Places *Ethan Frome* as an important part of Wharton's development as an author.

Walton, Geoffrey. *Edith Wharton: A Critical Interpretation.* 2d ed. Rutherford, N.J.: Fairleigh Dickinson University Press, 1982. Sees

Ethan Frome as a study of tragedy in middle-class life and criticizes the novel as "too inevitable." However, he does credit the novel with exploring the misery that can result from a devotion to such values as personal pride, desperate individualism, and conservatism.

Wershoven, Carol. *The Female Intruder in the Novels of Edith Wharton.* Rutherford, N.J.: Fairleigh Dickinson University Press, 1982. Many of Wharton's novels contain a female intruder who stands outside her society and forces other characters to reexamine their world. Mattie Silver could play this role in *Ethan Frome.*

Wolff, Cynthia Griffin. *A Feast of Words: The Triumph of Edith Wharton.* New York: Oxford University Press, 1977. A major addition to Wharton scholarship, which makes excellent use of psychoanalysis. Sees *Ethan Frome* as Wharton's exploration and rejection of her own repression.

Essays

Becker, May Lamberton. "Read This One First." *Scholastic* 31 (1937): 20-E.

Bernard, Kenneth. "Imagery and Symbolism in *Ethan Frome.*" *College English* 23 (1961): 178–84. Reprinted in Nevius, *Edith Wharton's "Ethan Frome."*

Blackall, Jean F. "The Sledding Accident in *Ethan Frome.*" *Studies in Short Fiction* 21 (1984): 145–46.

Brennan, Joseph. "*Ethan Frome*: Structure and Metaphor." *Modern Fiction Studies* 7 (1961–62): 347–56. Reprinted in Nevius, *Edith Wharton's "Ethan Frome."*

De Voto, Bernard. "Introduction to *Ethan Frome.*" New York: Charles Scribner's Sons, 1938. Reprinted in Nevius, *Edith Wharton's "Ethan Frome."*

Eggenschwiler, David. "The Ordered Disorder of *Ethan Frome.*" *Studies in the Novel* 9 (1977): 237–46.

Hamblen, Abigail Ann. "Edith Wharton in New England." *New England Quarterly* 38 (1965): 239–44.

Hays, Peter L. "First and Last in Ethan Frome." *Notes on Modern American Literature* 1 (1977): item 15.

Hovey, R. B. "'Ethan Frome': A Controversy about Modernizing It." *American Literary Realism* 19 (1986): 4–20.

Kazin, Alfred. "Afterward." In *Ethan Frome.* New York: Macmillan, 1987.

Leach, Nancy R. "New England in the Stories of Edith Wharton." *New England Quarterly* 30 (1957): 90–98.

MacCallan, W. D. "The French Draft of Ethan Frome." *Yale University Library Gazette* 27 (1952): 38–47.

Bibliography

Murad, Orlene. "Edith Wharton and Ethan Frome." *Modern Language Studies* 13 (1983): 90–103.

Nevius, Blake. "'Ethan Frome' and the Themes of Edith Wharton's Fiction." *New England Quarterly* 24 (1951): 197–207.

O'Neal, Michael J. "Point of View and Narrative Techniques in the Fiction of Edith Wharton." *Style* 17 (1983): 270–89.

Ransom, John Crowe. "Characters and Character: A Note on Fiction." *American Review* 6 (January 1936): 271–88. Reprinted in Nevius, *Edith Wharton's "Ethan Frome."*

Rose, Alan Henry. " 'Such Depths of Sad Initiation': Edith Wharton and New England." *New England Quarterly* 50 (1977): 423–39.

Saunders, Judith P. "Becoming the Mask: Edith Wharton's Ingenues." *Massachusetts Studies in English* 8 (1982): 33–39.

Shuman, R. Baird. "The Continued Popularity of *Ethan Frome*." *Revue des Langues Vivantes* 37 (1971): 257–63.

Thomas, J. D. "Marginalia on *Ethan Frome*." *American Literature* 27 (1955): 405–9.

Tuttleton, James. "Edith Wharton, High Priestess of Reason." *Personalist* 47 (1966): 382–98.

Wolff, Cynthia Griffin. "Cold Ethan and 'Hot Ethan.'" *College Literature* 14 (1987): 230–44.

Bibliographies

Bendixen, Alfred. "A Guide to Wharton Criticism, 1976–1983." *Edith Wharton Newsletter* 2 (1985): 1–8.

———. "Recent Wharton Studies: A Bibliographic Essay." *Edith Wharton Newsletter* 3 (1986) 5, 8–9.

———. "Wharton Studies, 1986–1987: A Bibliographic Essay." *Edith Wharton Newsletter* 5 (1988): 5–8, 10.

Springer, Marlene. *Edith Wharton and Kate Chopin: A Reference Guide.* Boston: G. K. Hall, 1976.

Springer, Marlene, and Joan Gilson. "Edith Wharton: A Reference Guide Updated." *Resources for American Literary Study* 14 (1984): 85–111.

Zilversmit, Annette. "Appendix, Bibliographical Index." *College Literature* 14 (1987): 305–9.

Index

Index

Isolation, 80–81; studies on the effects of, 48–49

James, Henry: as friend, 5, 21, 25; as critic, 13, 24–25; illness of, 36–37, 39, 41
Jewett, Sarah Orne: contrasted to Wharton, 10, 15, 76, 77, 79–80
Job, 97
Jude Fawley, 43–44, 58

Kazin, Alfred, 45, 46; *On Native Grounds*, 18

Lapsley, Gaillard, 6
Lawson, Richard: *Edith Wharton*, 19
Lee, Vernon, 5
Lewis, Nancy: as co-editor of letters, 21–22
Lewis, R. W. B.: as biographer, 18–19, 22, 25, 37, 103; as co-editor of letters, 21–22

Lily Bart (*The House of Mirth*), 63–64
Lindberg, Gary: *Edith Wharton and the Novel of Manners*, 19
Lockridge, Richard, 103, 108, 110–11
Lodge, Elizabeth, 41
Lubbock, Percy, 21; as biographer, 18, 22; "The Novels of Edith Wharton," 14

McDowell, Margaret: *Edith Wharton*, 19
Mattie: childhood of, 71, 74; Ethan, parallels to, 74; Ethan, relationship with, 52–55, 70–75, 105–11; as fairy maiden, 70–75; and father's death, 71, 74, 93; future, fear of, 54,

72–75; as a fury, 96; name as symbolic, 93; Zeena, parallels to, 69, 70, 75; Zeena, relationship with, 49–51, 66–67, 68, 72, 107–11
Maupassant, Guy de, 14
Medicines, 61–63; in *The House of Mirth*, 63–64
Melville, Herman, 27; *Moby-Dick*, 79, 80
Mencken, H. L., 68

Narrator: and Ancient Mariner, 28; and Ethan, 27, 31, 80; personality of, 15, 27; role of, 15, 18, 24, 27–31, 105; and setting, 76–77, 79–80; and Wharton, 20, 25–31.
Narrative frame, 11, 24–29, 36, 102, 103; and Balzac, 26–27, 29; criticism, 14, 17, 18, 19, 20, 24–25, 82; dramatic adaptation, 102, 103; ellipsis, 28, 29, 57; and symbolism, 94; Wharton's comments on, 15, 25–26
Naturalism, 58
Nevius, Blake, 18
Nightmares, 11, 30, 42, 70, 103

Oliver, F. E., 62

Paris, 5, 7, 16, 36, 45
Penrod, Steven, 49
Phelps, William Lyon: *The Advance of the English Novel*, 14–15
Plato: *Symposium*, 48
Poverty, 2, 10, 44–46
Pulitzer Prize, 6, 103

Railroad, 81
Ransom, John Crowe, 18
Realism, 10, 15, 19

introduction to, 15–16,
24–25, 76, 101; *Ethan Frome*,
parallels to, 10, 19–20, 30–31,
36–41, 70; expatriation, 5;
father, relationship with, 3,
21; friends, 4, 5 (*see also* individual names); friendships,
attitude toward, 5, 19, 22; and
Fullerton, 6, 19, 22, 30, 36-
41; illness, 4, 22; letters and
papers, 5, 14, 16, 21–22, 37,
38, 41; marriage, 4, 6, 19, 36,
37–38, 39, 41; men, relationships with, 4, 5, 6, (*see also*
individual names); mother,
relationship with, 3, 20, 30;
and narrator, 20, 25–31; poetry, 3, 4, 6; publishers, 14, 21;
Pulitzer prizes, 6, 103;
reviews, attitude toward, 14;
and Sarah Orne Jewett, 10,
15, 76, 77, 79–80; and thresholds, 30, 31; travels, 4–5;
wealth, 3, 5, 16, 22, 45;
women, relationships with, 4

AUTOBIOGRAPHY
A Backward Glance 4, 6, 15, 16, 25,
96, 100
"Life and I," 3

DRAMA
The Old Maid, 103

NONFICTION
"The Writing of Ethan Frome," 25
The Writing of Fiction, 6

NOVELS
The Age of Innocence, 6, 14, 15
The Children, 25
The Custom of the Country, 6, 19, 25
The Gods Arrive, 25

The House of Mirth, 4, 9, 14, 19,
63–64
The Reef, 14
Summer, 6, 25
The Valley of Decision, 19, 25

POETRY
"Terminus," 39

SHORT STORIES
"The Bunner Sisters," 6
"Mrs. Manstey's View," 4

UNPUBLISHED WORKS
"Beatrice Palmato," 21
The Buccaneers, 6

Wharton, Edward, ("Teddy"):
depressions, 5, 37, 38, 41;
divorce, 5, 38; as father figure,
37; marriage, 4, 6, 19, 36,
37–38, 39, 41; *Ethan Frome*,
parallels to, 19, 38–39, 70
Wilkins, Mary, 15
Wolff, Cynthia Griffin, 37; "Cold
Ethan and 'Hot Ethan,'"
35–36, 41; *A Feast of Words:
The Triumph of Edith
Wharton*, 19–20, 21, 30–31,
39, 45, 55; "Introduction" to
Ethan Frome, 29–30
Women: economic conditions of,
72–74
Woolf, Virginia, 4
Writing: early attempts, 3, 4; earnings from, 5; habits, 4

Zeena: and community, 60–61, 64;
as Ethan's conscience, 47, 57,
96; Ethan, relationship with,
47–52, 64–70, 105–11; as
financial drain, 50–51, 66–67;
as a fury, 96; and hysteria,
65–66; illness of, 50–51, 72,

The Author

Marlene Springer is professor of English and vice chancellor for academic affairs at East Carolina University in Greenville, North Carolina. A specialist in nineteenth century American and British literature, Professor Springer earned her Ph.D. from Indiana University in 1970. Her books include *Edith Wharton and Kate Chopin: A Reference Guide* (1976) and *Thomas Hardy's Use of Allusion* (1983); she is the editor of *What Manner of Woman: Essays on English and American Life and Literature* (1977; translated into Japanese by Fukoko Kabayoshi, 1985); and, with Haskell Springer, *Plains Woman: The Diary of Martha Farnsworth* (1986).